America, Wake Up!

We are Destroying the American Economy and Ourselves

Volume I

Bright Harry

ISBN-13:978-1466449916
ISBN-10:1466449918

DEDICATION

I dedicate this book to my late loving and great mother, Catherine Harry, who instilled in me to always look at the bigger picture --- to have a panoramic view of life ---- and then zoom down to the details.

Even more important is my wonderful, junior sister, Helen and her two beautiful and brilliant daughters, Tina and Elaine. Without their love, support and encouragement, this book would not have been written.

Finally, I also dedicate this book to my late Business Partner, Lally Locke, a prolific Inventor who died with her dreams of more than 300 fascinating inventions that would have made the world, especially the United States, much better. She died looking for funds to produce and market her inventions in the most capitalist country in the world, the United States, but found no capital. No capital in the most capitalist country in the World for Entrepreneurs. What an irony.

All these women were instrumental to my crafting this first volume and more to come. May the souls of my late Mother, Catherine and my late Business Partner, Lally rest in peace. You'll not be forgotten.

CONTENTS

at large.

What will the United States be like if this phony Government Budget Deficit Achilles Hill is removed from our American Psyche?

Chapters of the Upcoming Volume II

Chapters Ten through Thirteen are for the upcoming Volume II of this book. A brief summary of each chapter is included here for lucidity and better comprehension of this first Volume.

What Exactly is Money and What is Real Wealth?
Phony Budgets Deficits and Real Deficits

Bright Harry's Economics Principles of Balance

Institutions

Revolutionary Democratic Capitalism

ACKNOWLEDGMENTS

I thank my housemate and friend, Ronald Draper, to whom I bounced off many of my ideas and who questioned my thoughts, thereby making me simplify the contents of this book for more lucidity.

PREFACE

As I was penning the last few words of this book in the first week of November 2011, the following headlines were screaming out loud all across the global news media.

"Greek government teeters, euro zone crisis deepens after referendum news.

'The crisis ... has taken on uncontrollable dimensions and is threatening the cohesion of Greek society,' says one lawmaker".

"Greek euro threat looms over Cannes G20 summit".

"Greek government on the brink of collapse.

PM Papandreou reportedly on verge of offering resignation; crisis overshadows meeting of G-20 in Cannes".

"Analysis: Leaving the euro carries massive costs".

"Greece prime minister struggles to form coalition.

Papandreou wins confidence vote on a pledge that he's willing to quit".

Greece is collapsing economically as is Italy, and as would many European countries, and eventually every single country on earth, including the United States because of a global monumental fraud called Government Budget Deficit and National Debt. There is no financial statement in Accounting or Economics called budget deficit, and the so-called national debt made up of the cumulative annual budget deficits over the years, is pure fallacy.

This profound human stupidity and very bad idea called Government Budget Deficit with its companion National Debt --- both extremely deadly ---- will decimate the economic lives of hundreds of millions of people throughout the World, especially in the United States.

My focus in this book is on the United States but the principles enunciated apply to all Nations. I am rushing this book for publication because of the December 23, 2011 the United States Congress imposed on itself, as a result of the failure of the Super-Committee, to come up with a plan to reduce the Federal Budget Deficit and National Debt. The failure of the Super-committee to come up with a consensual decision, will now trigger the automatic across the board spending cuts of $1.2 Trillion.

It's no surprise that the Super-committee failed to come to a consensus by deadline of Noveber 23, 2011, , thereby triggering the across the board spending cuts that will decimate the already fragile American economy --- a monumental disaster in the making.

They were simply chasing phantoms, an action in futility, for there is nothing like Federal Budget Deficit and there is no National Debt. Yes, there is a gap between what the Government receives in Taxes and what it spends, and when the Expenditure is larger than the Tax Receipts, the Government claims to have a Budget Deficit. These cumulative annual Budget Deficits over the years are what we claim as National Debt.

This gap between Government Expenditure and Government Revenue is not a budget deficit but a consciously chosen budgetary shortfall by the Government. A mere gimmick. For the Government decides how much tax to collect and how much to spend. Taxes are mandatory and hence, the Government can always raise enough taxes to balance the amount it intends to spend. It's that simple. Thus, there is nothing like a Federal Budget Deficit and nothing like a National Debt. The Super-committee just wasted tax payers money and time on a fool's errand.

My intent for this hurried publication is to educate the American public, "We the People", who would then take prompt action with regards to this phony budget deficit and illusory national debt, to prevent the pending and unnecessary economic catastrophe, that will turn the present Great Recession of 2007 into the 21st Century Great Depression, as was the case in 1929. Hence, my wake up call to every American.

Yes, America, Wake Up! Wake Up from your slumber of not knowing what to do about the economy or more precisely, your ignorance. Wake Up from your lethargy and confusion about the economy. Wake Up from your gloom and doom. Just Wake Up and realize that no aliens from Mars or Saturn caused the present economic collapse and financial quagmire on Earth, especially in the United States.

You and I are the cause of the present economic crisis in the United States and globally, through our silence, inaction or passivity. We have allowed others, be they deficit hawks, the White House, US Congress, Lobbyists, Tea Partiers or what have you, dictate our economic future for us. We have abdicated from our sovereign rights to control our lives, economy and future, individually and collectively.

Our individual and collective thoughts, words and deeds create our future and whatever we want, including the type of economic system. We created the present economic crisis as it is and we are the only ones who can use this crisis opportunity to transform our present Feudalistic and Plutocratic Capitalism, to a truly Revolutionary Democratic Capitalism for all Americans, not just the few Wealthy Elites and the well-connected. We must ensure that every American is groomed as a Capitalist to democratize Capitalism and re-democratize America, thereby continuing to make the United States the beacon of light, hope and prosperity to the rest of the World. We must stop practicing Capitalism without Capitalists. In short, we must democratize our present Feudalistic and Plutocratic Capitalism to meet the demands of the 21st century knowledge economy. For our present economic model is totally broken and destroying us. And we are the only ones who can force into play and then execute this economic transformation.

Who are the "We"? We the People. The preamble to our American Constitution did not say, "We the White House", "We the Congress", "We the Legislators", "We the Judiciary", "We the Corporations", "We the Lobbyists", "We the Wealthy Elite" or "We the Budget Deficit Hawks". It states very simply and clearly, "We the People" ---- for sovereign power belongs only to "We the People".

Hence, "We the People" must exercise our sovereign power to take control of our future, our lives and our economy, especially from the "Budget Deficit Hawks", who are the cause of the present Great Recession that is not only getting worse but has already decimated millions of American lives, and many more worldwide.

America, Wake Up!

We are Destroying the American Economy and Ourselves

Yes, our fear of the Government Budget Deficit is presently our biggest problem. And our attempts at reducing this Federal Budget Deficit, with the ultimate aim of balancing the Budget and paying off the National Debt is the deadliest game we are playing.

This book in your hands will prove to you once and for all, that the Government Budget Deficit and National Debt are not just phantoms but monumental frauds, decimating American lives all over our beloved country.

INTRODUCTION

It was a balmy day with the bright California sun streaming down from the heavens and showering the earth with its golden rays. Golden rays of sunshine in the Golden State with the white clouds in the sky occasionally abruptly interrupted by light blue color. It was a beautiful sight to behold. Just one of those days in Fremont, California when the weather looked perfect, warm and cozy. A gorgeous Saturday on July 16, 2011.

Wearing a white T-shirt and grey jogging pants, just right for the great weather, I walked calmly along Walnut Street towards Fremont Boulevard, enjoying the light breeze and warmth of the sun on my skin.

And suddenly, I saw a black object by the sidewalk, beside a grocery cart with a blue suitcase on top of it. As I got closer accelerating my pace to satisfy my curiosity, I realized the black object was a human being lying on the sidewalk, under the shade of a tree, just in front of "Aegis Living", a retirement home for Seniors. On reaching the target, I saw a beautiful and fair-complexioned African-American lady, probably in her early thirties and wearing a superb black linen dress but lying down on the ground by the grocery cart with the light blue suitcase.

Stunned at what I saw and very alert, I could hear birds chirping in the trees above us, as cars zipped back and forth on both sides of Walnut Street. Confused but still thinking fast, I immediately flipped my cell phone out of my pocket to call 911 but realized that she was breathing normally and looked quite healthy. I watched her very close for a couple of minutes and knew immediately that she was simply exhausted and also a newly homeless, carrying her few belongings in her blue suitcase.

Tears welled down my eyes as I kept looking at the woman and scene, still confused at what to do. Should I wake her up and question her or call 911? After much thought, I decided to continue walking to the Department Store, Target, just across Fremont Boulevard to pick up some items with the intention of checking the lady again on my way back.

After about an hour, I arrived back at the scene and the lady was gone. I felt relieved that she was ok but at the same time I was saddened by the fact that Americans and Californians for that matter, would be homeless in this 21st Century. It was just too hard to swallow.

As I was walking back home, reminiscing, I started recalling the homeless European-American female I occasionally see along Fremont Boulevard pushing two grocery carts at the same time, with all her belongings. Then, I remembered the fifty-something year old European-American male I once in a while encounter on Central Avenue and Fremont Boulevard, sometimes at the Seven-Eleven, smoking and drinking bear, to while away his sorrows and time. He had a golf ball-sized lump on the left side of his forehead and always walked very slowly with a four-legged support. He was also homeless but quite normal like the Average American.

All these made me wonder and at times furious at the plight of our fellow human beings we ignore in the name of Budget Deficits and all worth not. It seems we value money more than life, forgetting that food, shelter and clothing existed long before the invention of money, a mere coupon, an IOU. And the so-called Budget Deficit is all about money, nothing more.

The plight of these homeless, penniless and confused human beings, Americans, in our midst forced me to spend enormous amount of my money, energy and resources for the past four years looking for an answer to the American economic system that is destroying the very fabric of our families, our communities, our society as a whole and our environment.

What I found out and still finding out are simply mind-numbing. My goal is to inform you through this book, for knowledge is potential power but applied knowledge is real power. I am waking us up from our ignorance starting with the Federal Budget Deficit and National Debt ---- both a monumental fraud, destroying everything in our beloved country. By the time you finish this book, this monumental fraud called Government Budget Deficit with its companion. National Debt will be as clear to you as night and day.

For now, just take a look around you. We have everything in the United States ----- good food, beautiful homes, running water, efficient telecommunication systems, constant electricity, good roads, good schools, functional sewer systems, sea ports, airports, great parks, some of the best technologies in the world, all types of consumer goods (Cars, TVs, Radios, Computers, Cell phones, and more), and whatever one actually desires. We also have all types of professionals, engineers, doctors, lawyers, professors, scientists, economists, plumbers, machinists, nurses, teachers, police, firefighters and you name it

In short, there is little or nothing that we lack in the United States in terms of human capital (manpower and womanpower), and goods and services. We also have all types of firms ready to produce these goods to satisfy our needs or desires.

Why then are Americans losing their homes to foreclosures and hundreds of thousands of Americans, if not millions, homeless in the midst of hundreds of thousands of empty homes? Something is awfully wrong here. Empty homes and homeless Americans!

America, Wake Up!

We are Destroying the American Economy and Ourselves

There are unsold cars in the auto dealerships, while many Americans are in need of such cars or even better ones. But the cars stay wasted in the parking lots unsold. The story is the same for most goods and services ---- sitting on the shelves but no buyers or customers.

As a result, the companies that produce these goods and services start to cut back and lay off more working Americans because there is no demand for their goods and services. A vicious circle of poverty begins with no end in sight, accompanied by the decimation of our families, communities, cities and crumbling infrastructure --- roads, bridges and more.

We are all sitting and watching helplessly as our bridges collapse, our roads deteriorate, our schools and educational system fail, our levees break apart and millions of Americans rendered homeless, penniless and hopeless, while millions more join the unemployment ranks. Hunger, poverty, anger, indebtedness and desperation seem to be the order of the day. All because of our fear of the Federal Government Budget Deficit and National Debt, that are exacerbating the present Great Recession, which started in 2007.

This Great Recession did not destroy any homes, businesses, people, forests, parks, infrastructure ---- roads, bridges, airports, seaports, rail lines, etc. Some of these assets may have changed ownership, but they are still the same assets before and after the economic crisis. The only difference is that banks, people and businesses ran out and still continue to run out of cash or money. Nothing more! Those with the cash become the new owners.

The questions that kept revolving in my mind were the following. What is the underlying cause of all these booms and bursts, with resultant massive poverty in the midst of abundance? How and why is the American economic model creating such monumental wretchedness and penury, while destroying our environment and the fabric of our families, communities and society as a whole? Why is the middle class being decimated, thereby creating a society of "have mores" and "have nothings"? Is there a better economic model that can mitigate these problems?

Yes, there is a superior economic model, not just a better one. This was what I found out in my four-year fascinating research, besides the fraud called Government Budget Deficit and National Debt. Quite exhilarating and enlightening. Our American Capitalist System is massively flawed and the founding Fathers foresaw it but could not correct it because of politics. It is the unfinished American Business.

"The Unfinished American Business" is my upcoming book I am still writing to pass on the knowledge I garnered in my intensive research to you and every American. As a matter of fact, to every person in this world because it applies to all humanity and to every Nation on earth. This book you reading this very moment is the first of three volumes being rushed for publication to ameliorate the present economic quagmire and pending cataclysmic economic catastrophe.

This volume I in your hands turns economics on its head, starting with the aforementioned Government Budget Deficit ----- the bone of contention between Budget Deficit Hawks or Fiscal Conservatives who want to rein in deficit and Progressives or Keynesians who want the Government to stimulate the economy through deficit spending.

Although Keynesians are closer to the truth about deficit spending to stimulate the economy, both Fiscal Conservatives and Keynesians are wrong about the Budget Deficit, because there is nothing like Government Budget Deficit. It is phony, non-existent

and in fact, an economic fraud, as stated earlier. I am yet to find the inventor of Government Budget Deficit or is it Nation's Budget Deficit.

Let's now go on an exciting and fascinating journey of imagination where there is no Government Budget Deficit. We have all the money in the world to do what we want --- turn our educational systems into the 21st century technological marvel, go to Mars and even Saturn if possible, provide wired and wireless broadband to every American home, ensure that every American family has a beautiful home, nice cars, great food, clean water to drink, and clean, safe and progressive communities, plus more. Besides, we now have the fastest, most modern and most efficiently integrated transportation system by air, sea and land, in the world. This of course includes the fastest and most efficient bullet trains plying all across America.

Stop dreaming for this is real. There is no Government Budget Deficit. We the people must wake up from our ignorance, NOW. This economic fraud called Budget Deficit is depriving us of all the above dreams and it has lasted for hundreds of years. Let's not allow it to last thousands of years, as was the case with Phlebotomy or Bloodletting, the one-size-fits-all-cure that killed hundreds of millions of human beings, if not a few billion, including our first President, George Washington.

Thus, carefully read this Volume I in your hands, understand it and then lead to liberate every American from this budget deficit economic fraud. For when the people lead, the leaders follow. It is not the other way round.

The liberation of the United States from the British Empire was started by the people, the ordinary citizens, before the founding

Fathers joined the revolution. So, let this economic revolution start with us, "we the people", and let the leaders follow.

Again, read, understand and then spread this knowledge, especially the following Economics Balancing Principles I have propounded:

BRIGHT HARRY'S ECONOMICS PRINCIPLES OF BALANCE

1. The Balancing Principle of Money only

a	Household Income	=	Household Expenditure
b	Business Income	=	Business Expenditure
c	Government Income	=	Government Expenditure
d	Nation's Income	=	Nation's Expenditure

In each of the above Formulas, we are simply balancing money with money, nothing more. Each component of each Equation above is an input to either the credit side or debit side of the Double-Entry Bookkeeping System in Accounting. Each of the incomes on the left goes to the Credit side of the ledger and each of the Expenditures on the right goes to the Debit side.

The main purpose of the Double-Entry Bookkeeping System in Accounting and Economics is to check errors, or imbalance. This means the incomes on the left must always balance the Expenditures on the right, for accuracy. In other words, the Debits must always balance the credits to ensure accuracy of data input into the fundamental Accounting Equation of Balance.

Now, only Formula 1d can stand on its own as will be explained more fully in Chapter 11, page 1. Not a single one of Formulas 1a, 1b or 1c can stand on its own. As such, each component of each Formula is incorporated into either the debit or credit side of the fundamental Accounting Equation of Balance, the Balance Sheet;

Assets = Liabilities + Owner's Equity

This is the most fundamental Formula in Accounting, Economics or Business that gives the true economic well-being or rather the true financial health of any entity. Similarly, Formula 1d which can also stand on its own, as will be fully explained throughout this Volume and in the upcoming Volume II, also gives the true economic health of any entity. It is also a very important Formula and Balancing Principle that can make or break a Nation.

2. The Balancing Principle of Real Money Supply and Real Wealth

Real Money Supply = Real Wealth

where Real Money Supply is the actual amount of money in circulation in the hands of Consumers

3. The Balancing Principle of Real Total Spending and Real Wealth

Real Total Spending = Real Wealth

where Real Total Spending is the actual amount of money spent in the Real Economy or Main Street, not speculation on Wall Street.

4. **The Optimum Balancing Principle or Equilibrium of Real Money Supply, Real Total Spending and Real Wealth**

Real Money Supply = Real Total spending = Real Wealth

These simple but profound economic principles of balance are lucidly described throughout this first Volume and expanded much further in volume II.

These Principles aside, I challenge any human being on this earth to disprove my postulations, clearly spelled out on the last page of this book, entitled "My Global Challenge" or on my website, AmericaWakeupSite.com. The first person who does this, will receive my first $25,000 profit from the sale of this book. Just ensure that you read the whole book before responding, so that we do not waste each other's time. For there is no National Budget Deficit and no National Debt.

Once more, our individual and collective thoughts, words and deeds make the America of our dreams. I am giving you my factual thoughts based my extensive and intensive research. Let's make them our individual and collective thoughts, words and deeds to build the America we want. I have done my part by providing you the information you are presently reading. What you do next with this knowledge is up to you and hence, to us all collectively.

America, Wake Up!

Let's Stop Destroying the American Economy and Ourselves because of Our Ignorance

Our ignorance of the Federal budget deficit and National debt has so mesmerized us, like hypnotized cobra under the spell of the Budget Deficit Charmers, that we watched helplessly in silence, wringing our hands in anguish, while sweating, as the Nation hurtled towards cataclysmic default implosion on August 2, 2011 --- a Nation held hostage and spellbound by the Deficit Hawks.

CHAPTER ONE

A NATION HELD HOSTAGE AND SPELLBOUND BY THE DEFICIT HAWKS

Tick Tock! Tick Tock! Tick Tock! Tick Tock! continued the time bomb as the 12:00 midnight deadline of Tuesday, August 2, 2011 approached fast. America and the world at large held their breath as the dysfunctional United States Congress fought over raising a debt limit that had nothing to do with the Federal Budget Deficit or the National Debt. The debt limit increase was to ensure that the United States Government paid its past bills or past financial obligations incurred by the same Congress. A traumatized Nation still in the throes of the Great Recession of 2007, held hostage and spellbound by the Deficit Hawks, because of a phony Federal Budget Deficit and the illusory National Debt.

After months of hair-raising haggling, more akin to a childish food fight than governance, the Legislators finally came to a consensus to beat the midnight deadline of August 2, 2011 and President Obama signed the Debt Limit Bill into Law. Much ado about nothing, but a monumental error on the part of the young president trying to compromise with recalcitrant ideologues, steeped in deep beliefs of budget deficit reduction and even the more lethal budget balance amendment, they want entrenched in the Constitution. President Obama would have been better off invoking the fourteenth amendment, than acceding to the rigid demands of these deficit hawks and signing the Debt Limit Act into Law.

It seems Washington DC has a very short memory – the Graham-Rudman-Hollings budget balancing amendment that failed woefully, has already been forgotten.

This Budget Balancing Amendment is briefly described below as culled from Wikipedia.[1]

Gramm–Rudman–Hollings Balanced Budget Act

"The **Gramm-Rudman-Hollings Balanced Budget and Emergency Deficit Control Act of 1985** (99th Congress, S.1702, Pub.L. 99-177, title II, December 12, 1985, 99 Stat. 1038, 2 U.S.C. § 900) and **Budget and Emergency Deficit Control Reaffirmation Act of 1987** (Pub.L. 100-119, title I, Sept. 29, 1987, 101 Stat. 754, 2 U.S.C. § 900) (both often known as **Gramm-Rudman**) were, according to U.S. Senator Phil Gramm of Texas, "the first binding constraint imposed on federal spending, and its spending caps have become part of every subsequent U.S. budget. Together with a rapidly growing economy it produced the first balanced federal budget in a quarter of a century."

Senators Ernest Hollings (D-South Carolina), Warren Rudman (R-New Hampshire) and Phil Gramm (R-Texas) were the chief sponsors. The Acts were aimed at cutting the budget deficit, which at the time was the largest in history. They provided for automatic spending cuts (called "sequesters") if the deficit exceeded a set of fixed deficit targets. The House passed the bill 271-154 and the Senate 61-31, and President Ronald Reagan signed the bill on December 12, 1985.[1] On August 12, 1986, Representative Dan Rostenkowski introduced the Balanced Budget and Emergency Deficit Control Reaffirmation Act. The Senate passed the bill with two amendments 36-35, and the House approved the Senate's first amendment by voice vote but rejected the second amendment; the Senate receded that amendment by voice vote. President Reagan signed the bill on August 21.[2] The process for determining the amount of the automatic cuts was found unconstitutional in the case of Bowsher *v. Synar*, 478 U.S. 714 (1986) and Congress enacted a reworked version of the law in 1987.[3] Gramm-Rudman failed, however, to prevent large budget deficits. The Budget Enforcement Act of 1990 supplanted the fixed deficit targets".

This stupid, senseless and meaningless Graham-Rodman-Hollings Balanced Budget Act failed because the Government Budget is not the Nation's Budget and hence, Government Budget Deficit is not the Nation's Budget Deficit. Furthermore, the Government is not the Nation, and hence, Government Debt is not the Nation's Debt. In other words, there is no National Budget Deficit and no National Debt. The Budget Deficit Hawks are behaving like dogs chasing their tails.

The following is an overview of the Debt Limit Act of 2011 from Speaker John Boehner's Website:

Summary of the Revised Budget Control Act of 2011[2]

Washington (Aug 1)

The final agreement to cut spending and avoid default meets Republicans' criteria to (1) cut government spending more than it increases the debt limit; (2) implement spending caps to restrain future spending; and (3) advance the cause of a Balanced Budget Amendment – all without tax hikes on families and job creators. It is largely consistent with the bill House Republicans passed last Friday, and reflects the principles of Cut, Cap, & Balance. Here is more information on the measure:

NO TAX HIKES

Same as the House-passed bill, the measure includes no tax hikes, a key principle that Republicans have fought for since day one. As further protection against any tax hikes, the Joint Committee of

Congress (described below) will be scored on a current-law baseline. The committee would have to raise taxes by more than $3.5 trillion above today's rates before it would begin to count as 'deficit reduction.' Since that is unlikely, there is little chance the Joint Committee will produce a bill that increases taxes.

CUTS THAT EXCEED THE DEBT HIKE

The final agreement is the same as the House-passed bill by including spending cuts that would exceed the amount of the increased debt authority granted to the President. The bill would cut and cap discretionary spending immediately, <u>saving $917 billion over 10 years – as certified by the nonpartisan Congressional Budget Office CBO) – and raise the debt ceiling by less – $900 billion – to approximately February</u>. Congress must vote to cut spending FIRST. Then, the President may ask for debt authority of up to $900 billion, which will be subject to a vote of disapproval by the House and Senate that can be vetoed by the President.

CAPS TO CONTROL FUTURE SPENDING

The final agreement is the same as the House-passed bill by imposing spending caps that would establish clear limits on future spending and serve as a barrier against government expansion while the economy grows. Failure to remain below these caps will trigger automatic across-the-board cuts (otherwise known as sequestration). This is the same mechanism used in the 1997 Balanced Budget Agreement. The one difference between this and the House-passed bill: the House bill had a firewall that separated defense from non-defense spending. Now the firewall separates security spending from non-security spending. This would be for FY 2012 & 2013, and allows Republicans to protect defense funding while cutting other security spending, such as foreign aid.

BALANCED BUDGET AMENDMENT

The bill advances the cause of a Balanced Budget Amendment by requiring the House and Senate to vote on the measure after October 1, 2011 but before the end of the year, allowing the American people time to build sufficient support for this popular reform. This is the same as the House-passed bill. Also, similar to the House-passed bill, the measure authorizes the President to request a second tranche of debt limit increase of $1.5 trillion if the Joint Committee's proposal is enacted OR if a Balanced Budget Amendment is sent to the states.

ENTITLEMENT REFORMS & SAVINGS

The final agreement is the same as the House-passed bill by creating a 12-member Joint Committee of Congress that is required to report legislation – by November 23, 2011 – that would produce a proposal to reduce the deficit by at least $1.5 trillion over 10 years. Each chamber would consider the proposal of the Joint Committee on an up-or-down basis without any amendments by December 23, 2011. Similar to the House-passed bill, if the Joint Committee's proposal is enacted OR if a Balanced Budget Amendment is sent to the states, the President would be authorized to request a debt limit increase of $1.5 trillion. As further protection against any tax hikes, the Joint Committee will work off a current-law baseline. The committee would have to raise taxes by more than $3.5 trillion above today's rates before it would begin to count as 'deficit reduction.' Since that is unlikely, there is little chance the Joint Committee will produce a bill that increases taxes.

The final agreement sets up a new sequestration process to cut spending across-the-board – and ensure that any debt limit increase is met with greater spending cuts – IF the Joint Committee fails to achieve at least $1.2 trillion. If this happens, then the President may request up to $1.2 trillion for a debt limit increase (note: this is less than the $1.5 trillion cited above). Assuming the President is able to increase the debt limit by $1.2 trillion (contingent upon the congressional disapproval process), then across-the-board spending cuts would result that would equal the difference between $1.2 trillion and the deficit reduction enacted as a result of the Joint Committee.

The across-the-board spending cuts would apply to FYs 2013-2021, and apply to both mandatory and discretionary programs. The final agreement specifies that total reductions would be equally split between defense and non-defense programs. The across-the-board cuts would also apply to Medicare. However, several programs would be exempted from across-the-board cuts, including Social Security.

The sequestration process does NOT trigger increased revenues. It can only result in spending cuts, not tax increases.

It now appears, "We the People" will have to push to abrogate this dangerous Law, that will ultimately turn our present Great Recession into the 21st Century Great Depression. For there is nothing like the much touted Federal Budget Deficit and the more insidious National Debt. Mere illusions.

The irony of this whole saga about the so-called Federal Budget Deficit and National Debt is this. The United States Congress or more precisely the Legislators set the tax rates for all Americans ---- individuals and businesses. They also decide the amount of money the Government can spend. The same Legislators, give authority to the Treasury Department and Federal Reserve, to print sufficient money into circulation in the American economy.

Let's get this straight for once. The United States Congress controls how much tax it wants to levy on every American and how much it wants to spend in the economy. This means the United States Congress controls the Government Tax Receipts and Government Expenditure. In other words, it has the power to increase or decrease the amount of tax it imposes on Americans. The Legislators also control Government Expenditure.

Since,

Government Budget Deficit = Government Tax Receipts – Government Expenditure

where Government Tax Receipts are smaller than Government Expenditure; the Government can always balance its Tax Receipts with its Expenditure at its discretion. It has full control over both component parameters making up the Budget Deficit.

Why then does the United States Congress not raise taxes on American citizens and businesses high enough to balance the Government Budget and even the National Debt, if that is what it wants?

Even better, why does the Government not print sufficient money into circulation, to balance the Federal Budget and the National Debt? Oh yes, most economists will shout inflation, inflation, inflation, while the Deficit Hawks will be on the verge of heart attack --- that we are hurtling towards Weimar-Germany.

Absolute nonsense. There will be no inflation and there will be no hyperinflation like Weimar-Germany. The US Government should print more money into circulation in the hands of Consumers, while reducing the tax burden on Americans --- individual citizens

and businesses. Inflation, especially Demand-Pull inflation is caused by too much money chasing too few goods. We have an abundance of goods and services in the United States. We lack nothing except cash, money or capital credit to buy these goods and services we have already produced, and now going to waste.

We must no longer allow this waste to continue. The US Government should stop making money scarce. Instead, it should ensure that the Treasury Department in conjunction with the Federal Reserve print sufficient money and circulate it into the Real Economy through the hands of Real Consumers. In other words, the Government should ensure that the amount of money in circulation in the hands of Real Consumers matches the Real Wealth of goods and services already on our shelves.

This is the single most important Economics Balancing Principle --- balancing Real Money in Circulation in the hands of Consumers with the Real Wealth of goods and services we have already produced. Putting it in mathematical form,

Real Money in circulation in Consumers' hands = Real Wealth

This simple but profound Economics Balancing Principle is the panacea to the present Great Recession of 2007, and is explained succinctly throughout this book.

With this knowledge in our pockets, let's toss out our toga of ignorance and wrap ourselves around "Knowing" to really know instead of being ensconced in the 'illusion of knowing", thereby deceiving ourselves, especially with regards to the so-called Government Budget Deficit ---- a phantom, a monumental fraud.

Read on..............

CHAPTER TWO

"KNOWING" AND THE "ILLUSION OF KNOWING"

Turn on your Television or Radio, surf the Internet, open your favorite Magazine or Newspaper, and you will be bombarded by the shrills of the all-knowing economic experts --- the Budget Deficit Hawks ---- about the profligacy of Washington DC and the coming bankruptcy of the United States due to Government Budget Deficit. These Budget Deficit Hawks have raised the decibel level to such a crescendo that the White House and Congress have set up a Super-committee to resolve this Budget Deficit Brouhaha once and for all. In fact, the biggest game in town is the reduction of this Government Budget Deficit and the National Debt.

Now, there is "knowing" and there is the "illusion of knowing". Science and engineering study nature --- real life, and then craft mathematical equations to match the natural phenomenon, while building models or systems to mimic the real life situation or nature. This is "knowing" through the study of nature.

On the other hand, Economics tries to fit real life situations --- real life economics --- into its bizarre econometric models, convoluted mathematical equations and meaningless economic theories; the "illusion of knowing".

These deficit hawks, economic experts, economic professors, economic pundits, economic gurus and even economic "wanna-bes" are all ensconced in the "illusion of knowing Government Budget Deficit or Nation's Budget Deficit" instead of actually "knowing the Real Deficit".

They force-fit the entire economic health of a nation into a very simple but extremely deadly Formula,

Nation's Budget Deficit = Government Revenue – Government Expenditure

And somehow, conventional economics has convinced every nation on Earth that Government Expenditure must always match Government Revenue for the nation to be fiscally prudent or even solvent. It is the Economic theory or law, all over the world, at present.

This was why FDR warned Americans in 1932 to be wary of man-made economic Laws.

"But while they prate of economic laws, men and women are starving. We must lay hold of the fact that economic laws are not made by nature. They are made by human beings".[1]

---------- *Franklin D. Roosevelt*

Who made this Economic Theory, Postulation or even Law that

Government Budget Deficit = Nation's Budget Deficit

and

Nation's Budget Deficit = Government Revenue – Government Expenditure

where, Government Expenditure is greater than Government Revenue?

This is the crux or the very essence of this book, to prove once and for all, the fallacy, deceit, lies and outright fraud that

Government Budget Deficit = Nation's Budget Deficit

and that there is even a "thing" called Nation's Budget Deficit.

Furthermore, I assert and will prove beyond any reasonable doubt that the Formula,

Nation's Budget Deficit = Government Revenue – Government Expenditure

is not just illusory and monumentally fraudulent but very deadly, and presently destroying the economy of every single Nation on Earth, including that of the United States. But before delving into the nitty-gritty, I am providing you with some quotations and statements about the so-called Nation's Budget Deficit, or is it Government Budget Deficit, from prominent Americans.

President Obama:

"What my budget does is to put forward some tough choices, some significant spending cuts, so that by the middle of this decade, our annual spending will match our annual revenues. We will not be adding more to the national debt," he said when asked about the GOP criticism. "We're not going to be running up the credit card anymore."[2]

-------------- *President Obama*

"The government had spent more money than it takes in for year and result was a lot of debt on our nation's credit card."

This debt would **"weaken our economy, cause higher interest rates for families, and force us to scale back things like education and Medicare"** unless action was taken.[3]

------------- *President Obama*

"For the last decade, we have spent more money than we take in. In the year 2000, the government had a budget surplus. But instead of using it to pay off our debt, the money was spent on trillions of dollars in new tax cuts, while two wars and an expensive prescription drug program were simply added to our nation's credit card.

As a result, the deficit was on track to top $1 trillion the year I took office. To make matters worse, the recession meant that there was less money coming in, and it required us to spend even more — on tax cuts for middle-class families; on unemployment insurance; on aid to states so we could prevent more teachers and firefighters and police officers from being laid off. These emergency steps also added to the deficit.

Now, every family knows that a little credit card debt is manageable. But if we stay on the current path, our growing debt could cost us jobs and do serious damage to the economy. More of our tax dollars will go toward paying off the interest on our loans. Businesses will be less likely to open up shop and hire workers in a country that can't balance its books. Interest rates could climb for everyone who borrows money — the homeowner with a mortgage, the student with a college loan, the corner store that wants to expand. And we won't have enough money to make job-creating investments in things like education and infrastructure, or pay for vital programs like Medicare and Medicaid."[4]

------------ *President Barack Obama*

Senator Mitch McConnell

"Well, what was wrong with it last year?" McConnell said to King. "I mean, I discussed this very issue with the president right after he came to office, and with his chief of staff. Never could get a commitment out of him. In the meantime, we've seen a year now in which we've been on a spending binge. They passed a budget that doubled the national debt in five years and tripled it in 10. There's a lot of skepticism now about whether -- and the president endorses this commission a couple of days before the vote [on the debt-limit bill]. Where was he a year ago when we were talking to him about it?"[5]

-------------*Mitch McConnell*

"My main criteria for selecting members was to identify serious, constructive senators who are interested in achieving a result that helps to get our nation's fiscal house in order," McConnell said in a separate statement. "That means reforming entitlement programs that are the biggest drivers of our debt, and reforming the tax code in a way that makes us more competitive and leads to more American jobs."[6]

-------------*Mitch McConnell*

Rep. John Boehner

"Runaway spending is another factor hobbling business confidence in the future, he said, adding that a joint congressional committee should focus on restraining deficits through spending cuts, not tax hikes". "That has everything to do with jobs"[7]

------------*John Boehner*

Washington (Mar 5, 2009) In his weekly press briefing this afternoon, House Republican Leader John Boehner (R-OH) highlighted Washington Democrats' out-of-control spending binge and the impact it is having on American families and small

businesses. Boehner criticized the "cramdown" housing bill Democrats brought to the House floor today — legislation that forces homeowners who played by the rules to reward scam artists, speculators, and those who made irresponsible decisions when purchasing a home. He also renewed his call for President Obama to veto the $410 billion "omnibus" spending bill loaded with 9,000 earmarks, discussed the first meeting of a solutions group he is leading to develop Republican solutions to help Americans rebuild their 401(k), college, and home savings, and talked about today's White House "Health Care Summit." Key excerpts and audio from Boehner's briefing follow:[8]

Rep. Eric Cantor

His stand and statement on the disaster that followed Tropical Storm Irene, on the East Coast, with regards to the so-called Government Budget Deficit.

Last week, Mr. Cantor, the majority leader, said that any money the federal government spends to assist storm-damaged areas should be offset by cuts elsewhere in the budget.

"Yes, we are going to find the money," Mr. Cantor said in an interview with Fox News, referring to disaster aid. "We are just going to have to make sure there are savings elsewhere to continue to do so."

"Just like any family would operate when it's struck with disaster, it finds the money to take care of a sick loved one or what have you, and then goes without trying to buy a new car or an addition onto the house," he added.[9]

"Put simply, less government spending equals more private sector jobs."[10]

----------Eric Cantor on Friday, March 4th, 2011 in a press release

"The budget submitted by Obama will add more to the debt than the outstanding debt of the previous 43 presidents combined." [11]

----------Eric Cantor

Rep. Paul Ryan

For the past year, Washington's leaders have taken an already unsustainable budget outlook and made it far worse. They have exploited Americans' genuine economic anxieties to justify an unrelenting and wide-ranging expansion of government. Their agenda has included, among other things, a failed, debt-financed economic "stimulus"; an attempt to control the Nation's energy sector; increasing domination of housing and financial markets; the use of taxpayer dollars to seize part ownership of two nearly bankrupt auto makers; and, of course, the planned takeover of Americans' health care, already heavily burdened, manipulated, and distorted by government spending and regulation. This domineering government brings taxes, rules, and mandates; generates excessive levels of spending, deficits, and debt; leads to economic stagnation and declining standards of living; and fosters a culture in which self-reliance is a vice and dependency a virtue – and as a result, the entire country weakens from within.

Increasingly, Americans are rejecting this approach, and for good reason. But the status quo is not acceptable either. The Federal Government's current fiscal path is unsustainable: it leads to unprecedented levels of spending and debt that will overwhelm the budget, smother the economy, weaken America's competitiveness in the 21st

century global economy, and threaten the survival of the government's major benefit programs. The President and congressional Majority are only hastening America's march toward this reckoning, adding to trillions of dollars worth of unfunded liabilities, and accelerating the erosion of Americans' health care and retirement security. Their "progressivism" ironically points backwards – to a future in which America's best century is the past century.[12]

"The President's partisan speech and misguided proposals are disappointing, but not surprising. Having overseen an unprecedented surge in government spending – from his failed stimulus law, to the creation of new trillion-dollar health entitlements, to double-digit percentage increases in the budgets of many federal agencies – the President has finally admitted that he plans to send the bill for Washington's reckless spending straight to American businesses and families. A $1.6 trillion tax hike on job creators is never a good idea. But taking more money from private savers and investors, and giving it to the same government bureaucrats who brought us the Solyndra debacle, is an even worse idea – especially in a weak economy.

"Unfortunately, none of the President's proposals this year – from his February budget to his April budget speech, to his recommendations today – offers a credible plan to lift our crushing burden of debt while restoring economic growth. Instead of renewed prosperity, the President has offered us a plan for shared scarcity. The nation deserves better."[13]

---------- *Paul Ryan*

Congressional Budget Office, CBO

The United States is facing profound budgetary and economic challenges. At 8.5 percent of gross domestic product (GDP), the $1.3 trillion budget deficit that the Congressional Budget Office (CBO) projects for 2011 will be the third-largest shortfall in the past 65 years (exceeded only by the deficits of the preceding two years). This year's deficit stems in part from the long shadow cast on the U.S. economy by the financial crisis and the recent recession. Although economic output began to expand again two years ago, the pace of the recovery has been slow, and the economy remains in a severe slump. Recent turmoil in financial markets in the United States and overseas threatens to prolong the slump.

CBO expects that the recovery will continue but that real (inflation-adjusted) GDP will stay well below the economy's potential—a level that corresponds to a high rate of use of labor and capital—for several years. On the basis of economic data available through early July, when the agency initially completed its economic forecast, CBO projects that real GDP will increase by 2.3 percent this year and by 2.7 percent next year. Under current law, federal tax and spending policies will impose substantial restraint on the economy in 2013, so CBO projects that economic growth will slow that year before picking up again, averaging 3.6 percent per year from 2013 through 2016.[14]

You now have a snapshot of the beliefs of some of our prominent Americans, Politicians, Legislators and even Institutions about the Government Budget Deficit.

As shown in the previous pages, what matters to any Nation is the balancing principle of Real Money Supply and Real Wealth. In other words,

Real Money Supply = Real Total Spending = Real Wealth

and not the phony and irrelevant formula,

Government Tax Receipts = Government Expenditure

from which the Government Budget Deficit is derived.

Thus,

If you believe in Government Budget Deficit, you are destroying the American Economy and yourself.

If you believe in reducing the Government Budget Deficit, you are destroying the American Economy and yourself.

If you believe in balancing the Government Budget, you are destroying the American economy and yourself.

The following are the horrendous consequences of our belief and fear of the Government Budget Deficit and National Debt, and our attempts at not just reducing them, but trying to balance them.

1. Massive foreclosures nationwide resulting in millions of empty homes, blighted neighborhoods and millions of homeless Americans, some sleeping in their cars.

2. Millions of unemployed and underemployed Americans, whose unemployment benefits have run out or are running out.

3. Rapid deterioration of our communities and families as unemployment and failing businesses take their toll.

4. Stifling of Government funding of Research and Development in the Sciences, Technologies and Manufacturing that ushered in the Internet and other innovative inventions.

5. Contraction of businesses, folding up of businesses, fewer business startups, unoccupied commercial buildings and empty offices, and discouragement of entrepreneurialism due to lack of investment funds and customers.

6. Massive indebtedness of American families, leading to reduction in the demand for goods and services, which in turn contracts businesses and increases unemployment.

7. State and Local Governments going broke and laying off many civil servants --- teachers, firefighters and police ---- thereby making our neighborhoods and communities less safe, and worsening an already extremely bad recession.

8. Social Security Insurance, Unemployment Insurance, Medicaid, Medicare and Welfare, all going broke due to lack of funds.

9. Rapid deterioration of our infrastructure ---- roads, bridges, levees, seaports, airports, school buildings, parks, and more.'

10. Rapid collapse of our educational system, manufacturing industrial base and ecosystem, and the gutting of our robust research and development on space at institutions like NASA ---- all starved of funds.

11. The accelerated disappearance of pension funds and the few still in existence going broke.

12. You can add your own ideas because there are many more ills in our society caused by our belief and fear of the government budget deficit and national debt.

"The illusion of knowing' the Federal Budget Deficit and National Debt is even more pervasive in the "phantom Nation" called Washington DC and "alien empire" of Wall Street, where smoke and mirrors are the weapons of mass destruction, to slay the deadly Federal Budget Deficit and National Debt. Phantom lands

of unreality, where illusions slay illusions, leaving massive wrecks in the real world of people, on which these phantom lands of Washington DC and Wall Street are founded. No Main Street, no Wall Street, and no Washington DC. But those ensconced in the illusion of knowing, do not know this, and continue dismantling Main Street as we all hurtle towards economic Armageddon.

Despite these illusions or more precisely deceit, no one, including these deficit hawks has any doubt that cutting spending while raising taxes increases unemployment, reduces purchasing power of consumers, and leads to contraction of companies, thereby making a very bad recession much worse. Even then, these ignorant deficit hawks and their ignorant followers insist, persist and continue to cut spending while raising taxes.

Just like phlebotomy or bloodletting, the cure-all for all types of diseases which lasted for thousands of years, resulting in the deaths of hundreds of millions of human beings, if not a few billion, including the first American President, the budget deficit reduction or balancing the budget as a cure for the recession is not only a monumentally stupid idea but an extremely dangerous one. This senseless reduction of a Nation's Budget Deficit is today, laying waste human lives, properties and infrastructure all across the Unites States.

It now seems history is repeating itself but does history really repeat itself? It is rather more apt to say that human stupidity repeats itself, and it's repeating itself.

Between 1929 and 1932, the United States money supply shrunk sharply, as banks failed and bank deposits and commercial credits vanished. Furthermore, the actions of the Federal Reserve in conjunction with Congress and President Herbert Hoover reduced the Money supply by one-third, thereby destroying a third of the

Money circulating in the Real Economy. There was thus, a mismatch between the Money Supply and Real Wealth of already produced goods and services. There wasn't sufficient Money in Circulation in the hands of Consumers to purchase the already produced goods and services on the shelves.

Adding insult to injury, President Herbert Hoover proposed and Congress passed the Revenue Act of 1932 because they felt Deficit Reduction was the highest economic priority. This Act set in motion the largest tax increases in the history of the United States. They were trying to reduce the Federal Budget Deficit and National Debt with the ultimate aim of balancing both the Federal Budget and National Debt. Millions of American lives were devastated, and the struggling, fragile economy collapsed. This became the Great Depression of the 1930s.

Now, eighty years later, President Obama, the United States Congress and the Fed are attempting the exact same monumentally stupid and extremely dangerous mistake of the 1930's ---- reducing spending and raising taxes to reduce the so-called Federal Budget Deficit and National Debt with the ultimate goal of balancing the Government Budget and National Debt.

The mindboggling similarity of the Great Depression of 1929 and the Great Recession of 2007 is uncanny to say the least. Just as President Herbert Hoover signed into law, the Revenue Act of 1932, President Obama on August 2, 2011 signed into Law, the Budget Control Act of 2011. In both instances, to reduce the Federal Budget Deficit and National Debt with the ultimate intent of balancing the Budget and National Debt.

Similarly, just as the Financial Institutions and Corporations were bailed out in the Great Depression of 1929, leaving out the American masses to wallow in their misery, misfortune and poverty, the same Financial Institutions and large Corporations were bailed out during this Great Recession of 2007, leaving the American masses gasping for air and struggling to survive.

America, Wake Up!

We are Destroying the American Economy and Ourselves

Same situation, same circumstances, same conditions, same culprits and same victims but different actors doing the same thing 80 years apart.

History does not repeat itself, human stupidity does.

Unless we change economic course, we are all hurtling towards another Great Depression in this 21st century. And change economic course we must, unless we are suicidal.

The White House, Congress and the Federal Reserve can start the change by infusing more funds into the hands of Real American Consumers, not financial institutions or large Corporations, who would then use the funds to buy the available goods and services on our shelves, presently worth $14.93 Trillion (the 2011 GDP). The amount of money in circulation in the hands of Real Consumers must always match the Real Wealth of goods and services we have already produced, $14.93 Trillion as of this writing.

Better still, the US Congress should and must abrogate the Dodd-Frank Wall-Street Reform and Consumer Protection Act of 2010, which reduced the TARP spending cap from the initial $700 billion to $475 billion, and release this fund directly to American Consumers in the form of interest-free loans to pay their mortgages and save their homes from foreclosures; to the States to balance their budgets and stop laying off Teachers, Firefighters, Police and other Civil Servants, while boosting Unemployment Compensation and Medicare and Medicaid Payments; and the Federal Government itself boosting massive infrastructure rebuilding and building to employ tens of millions of Americans as FDR did during the Great Depression of 1929. This will be a first start towards our recovery from this horrendous Great Recession.

The only things stopping us from doing all the above are our belief and fear of the phony Government Budget Deficit and the illusory National Debt. Mere phantoms.

My intent for writing this book in your hands, is to provide you with solid facts and irrefutable knowledge, so that you can educate your families, your friends and your neighbors. Then go further to educate your Congressmen, your Senators and even the White House, from what you glean from this book, so that we can take back our economy, our country and our lives. For the Phony Budget Deficit is what is destroying the American economy and ourselves, and indirectly, the Global Economy.

All I ask of you is to be open-minded. Forget all your biases and previous ideas about budgets and budget deficits and try to comprehend what I am writing here. Then, you can draw your own conclusions. But I can assure you that by the time you read the last words and understand them thoroughly, you and I will come to the same conclusion, that the so-called Government Budget Deficit is phony and in fact, a fraud.

Then, you might ask the budget deficit economic gurus, pundits, charlatans and hawks, the following questions:

1. Who invented the Government Budget Deficit and why?

2. How have you been hurt receiving money from the Government?

3. How have you been hurt by the Government reducing your taxes?

4. How have you been hurt by the Government spending money to repair our bridges, roads and sewer systems, build new infrastructure, boost our education system and increase funding for research and development?

We are Destroying the American Economy and Ourselves

5. How have you or anyone you know been hurt by the Budget Deficit?

6. How is the Budget Deficit the most serious problem in the US today?

7. If the Government is not the Nation, why is the Government Budget Deficit the Nation's Budget Deficit?

8. Since the United States Congress sets the tax rates for all Americans and also decides how much money the Government can spend, why does the Congress not raise taxes high enough to match its expenditure? After all, Congress totally controls both component parameters of the Budget Deficit, Revenues and Expenditures.

9. Finally, what exactly is money and why do we make it scarce compared to our real wealth, being wasted in the form of foreclosed homes, unsold cars, empty offices, shuttered factories and unemployed professionals like engineers and lawyers? Why do we make money more important than life, when millions of Americans are homeless in the midst of hundreds of thousands or even a few million foreclosed and empty homes?

These are questions you should reflect on for now, but once you grasp the facts that I am putting in front of you, that the Government Budget Deficit is phony, the answers will be as clear to you, as night and day.

To understand this Budget Deficit, we must at least know what a Budget is. So, what exactly is a budget?

CHAPTER THREE

WHAT EXACTLY IS A BUDGET?

Just hearing the word "Budget", most people immediately think of Expenditure and Income. A little more reflection would reveal that this is not true. A budget has little or nothing to do with income. The Income is just a constraint or limiting factor to the Budget, which is simply a spending plan. Thus, what exactly is a budget?

A budget is an itemized spending plan constrained by time or maximum available financial or other resources. You budget your time because you have only 24 hours in the day and 365 days in the year, except for leap years, which have 366 days. You are prioritizing your activities with respect to time, to be more efficient or to achieve the most in the shortest possible time.

You also budget your money limited by how much you make or earn. You want to get the best bang for your money.

Companies budget their money constrained by how much money they have. They also budget their production limited by the availability of raw materials, funds and time. But most times, our budgeting is focused on money or our financial resources. As such, we will focus only on financial budgeting here.

Now, just as a family financial budget is different from a business financial budget, so is a business financial budget different from a government financial budget, which in turn is not the same as a nation's financial budget.

A family makes a budget for food, housing, clothing, education, transportation, entertainment and other necessities of life to first survive, and then thrive into leisure. It makes its budget

constrained by available or expected income. This is fiscal discipline and prioritizing, nothing more.

A business makes a budget for all its inputs of production --- buildings, raw materials, employee salaries, machines, water, electricity and more, within the limits of its available financial resources. This is also fiscal prudence, nothing more.

A government also makes a budget to pay judges, legislators, and in fact, all government employees, defense, military weapons, transfer payments --- Social Security Insurance, Unemployment Insurance, Medicare, Medicaid, and Foreign Aid, not excluding many others like emergency relief funds for disasters. This is also fiscal discipline to reduce unnecessary waste.

A nation also has a budget but it is totally different from that of the government. This is because the nation comprises of the social institutions --- Government, Households and Businesses. Hence, a Nation's Budget is the combined Budgets of the government, households and businesses. In other words,

A Nation's Budget = Government Budget + Households' Budgets + Businesses' Budgets

In short, a Government Budget is not a Nation's Budget. This fallacious assumption of equating a Government Budget to a Nation's Budget is the bane of the present global budgetary nightmare and economic collapse of nations all over the world. If the Government Budget is not the Nations' Budget, then the Government Budget Deficit is not the Nation's Budget Deficit.

What then is Budget Deficit?

Budget Deficit is defined as the shortfall in Revenue compared to Expenditure or the gap between the lesser Revenue and larger Expenditure. In other words,

Budget Deficit = Revenue – Expenditure

where, Expenditure is greater than Revenue. And hence,

Government Budget Deficit = Government Revenue – Government Expenditure

where, Government Expenditure is greater than Government Revenue.

This means that if the Government Expenditure is $3.83 Trillion in 2011 and expected Tax Receipt is $2.17 Trillion for the same year, it has a Budget Deficit of $1.66 Trillion for the year. This $1.66 Trillion Government Budget Deficit is phony and a mere spurious number as would be shown later. But how did budget deficit itself really originate?

What is the origin of this Budget Deficit?

Stating it another way, who invented this Budget Deficit that is presently decimating every single Nation on Earth?

I have researched as far back as the Egyptian Empire (5,000 BCE), Greek City States and even the Roman Empire, and so far come up empty handed. There is nothing like a budget deficit in past civilizations.

The only relevant information I stumbled on is the double-entry bookkeeping system or methodology, first documented by the Franciscan Friar of Italy, Luca Pacioli in 1494. He is credited as the founder of modern Accounting. Even in his treatise, there is nothing called budget deficit, just as there is nothing like budget

deficit in today's modern Accounting Financial Statements and double-entry bookkeeping.

Rather, the components of the so-called Budget Deficit, Revenues and Expenditures are respectively placed under Credit and Debit of the double-entry bookkeeping system to balance the core Accounting Equation,

Assets = Liabilities + Owner's Equity

This is the Balance Sheet and the Formula that counts. It depicts the economic well-being or financial health of any entity – household, business, government or even nation. No where in Economics or Accounting does the Formula for Budget Deficit,

Budget Deficit = Revenue – Expenditure

stand alone and used as the gauge for the economic health of any entity or institution. The Government Budget Deficit and National Debt are monumental frauds.

Now, it appears we human beings are confused, equating Fiscal Responsibility with Budget Deficit. As succinctly described earlier, reducing the Budget Deficit and National Debt or even Balancing the Budget and National Debt does not make a Nation economically healthy or even fiscally responsible. What then do we mean by Fiscal Responsibility?

Fiscal Responsibility

Assuming your best friend earns $60,000 annually and spent $80,000 for the year. According to our definition of budget deficit, your friend has a deficit of $20,000 for the year. Now, is she fiscally responsible? Is she going to be bankrupt? It all depends on the context of the budget deficit.

If she used the $20,000 to fly to Cancun, Hawaii, London and Paris to have fun and enjoy herself, without sufficient savings and no means of paying back the $20,000, then she is fiscally irresponsible and may even go bankrupt eventually, unless of course she has sufficient savings or residual equity or assets.

On the other hand, if she invests the $20,000 in a very lucrative business venture with great upside potential, she is fiscally prudent. The business may even fail but she is still fiscally prudent because starting a business is calculated risk-taking in life. If she succeeds in the business, she will reap more than she sowed with the $20,000 investment capital. That's fiscal prudence.

Similarly, if the Government borrows to finance long-term investments like education, renewable energy, research and development, and rebuilding our dilapidating infrastructure – roads, bridges, sewer systems, and even build new ones like mass transport systems, including bullet trains all across the United States, the Government is fiscally responsible.

On the other hand, if the Federal Government borrows to finance tax cuts for the wealthy or "have mores" and the "have mores" use the money to speculate on Wall Street, buy luxury Yachts and other ostentatious goods produced outside the shores of the United States, the Government is fiscally irresponsible.

What's important is not so much about how much the Government spends or how much tax it receives, but what it spends the money on. Is the Government spending for future wealth creation like infrastructure, education and research and development or for future poverty creation, like unnecessary wars and useless tax breaks for the filthy rich, who do not even need the extra money?

Let's now take a closer look at how the US Government spends our money and what it receives in the form of taxes to understand the so-called government Budget Deficit much better.

Government Expenditure

Government Expenditure which is actually the Budget, is the most contentious issue in the United States, especially among the Politicians. Fierce disagreements on Spending and Taxing shut down the Federal Government during Bill Clinton's Presidency and almost happened again in 2011 under Barack Obama's Presidency.

While Republicans are bent on reducing or even eliminating Taxes altogether and cutting Spending at the same time to balance the phony Federal Budget, the Democrats are more focused on increasing Taxes and Spending, also to balance the same phony Federal Budget Deficit. Futile actions that are of no relevance to the overall United States Economy. So, how and where does the Federal Government spend our money?

Let's take a closer look at how the $3.60 Trillion Government Expenditure for Fiscal Year 2011 is broken down.

From this $3.60 Trillion, 16% is for Pensions (Social Security, etc), 11% for Welfare, 15% for National Defense, 18% for Health Care (Medicaid and Medicare), 15% for Education and 6% for interest payment on the so-called National Debt. All these, total 81% of the Federal Expenditure for the Fiscal year 2011. The remaining 19% are for Transportation, Housing, Agriculture, Foreign Aid and miscellaneous expenses.

At the moment, the talk all over the Unites States is that the Government is facing a monumental crisis of Budget Deficit and

National Debt, in addition to accelerating entitlements that are on the verge of bankrupting the Nation. Hence, the Government needs to rein in the above itemized spending to avoid a similar collapse like the Greek Government. In short, the US Government is profligate and needs to reduce the itemized public spending just described.

It appears we are all going round and round in circles. We do not want our roads, bridges, levees, sewer systems and schools to fall apart but we do not want the Government to spend more to fix these crumbling assets. The questions we need to ask ourselves are the following:

1. How big do we want our Government to be?

2. What do we want the Government to do for us?

3. How are we going to pay for what we want the Government to do for us?

4. What are the limits of the Government?

By truthfully answering these questions, maybe we Americans will finally come to a reasonable solution. Until then, we are simply blowing hot air, and will continue complaining about the so-called Federal Budget Deficit, and the size and functions of Government. But what are the exact functions of our Federal Government?

The Constitution states that the Federal Government's role is "to provide for the general welfare". So, how do we interpret general welfare? What is included in our general welfare --- Infrastructure repair and development, education, research and development, defense, entitlements, bailing out too-large-to-fail institutions, universal health insurance --- or what? Until we decide what we mean by our general welfare and how we are going to pay for it, there is no answer to what and how much the Government should spend. But this expenditure has nothing to do with the

phony or fraudulent budget deficit and illusory national debt. It's just an Expenditure, constrained only by our Real Wealth of goods and services.

Furthermore, the Federal Spending breakdown described earlier is classified under three major categories of Government Spending.

a. **Discretionary spending**, are those within the 13 appropriations bills in the annual budget, and negotiated between the Branches of Congress and the President's Office each year. This is where politicians have more control and are not constrained as in Mandatory spending, which includes all spending not in the Discretionary spending.

b. **Mandatory spending**, also called entitlements is set in the law and hence, there is nothing the politicians can do unless they amend the law. This is where Social Security, Medicaid, Medicare, and Income Support programs like Food Stamps and Veterans Retirement programs fall in, and they are the largest components of the Federal Government spending. As such, these entitlements make up most the so-called budget deficits and national debt with accompanying interest payments.

c. **interest payments** on debt. This is the interest the Government pays on the so-called national debt.

Owing to the present Great Recession, TARP was also included in the Mandatory spending. In a nutshell, the above categories are where the US Governments spends most of its money called the annual budget.

This annual budget usually originating from the US President is sent to Congress, which eventually approves it because Congress controls the purse-strings of the Nation. Thus, the US Congress controls the Expenditure component of the Budget Deficit Formula,

Government Budget Deficit = Government Tax Receipts –
Government Expenditure

As shown below, Congress also controls the Revenue component of the same Budget Deficit Equation. This Revenue component is also the Tax Receipts or

Government Revenue = Government Tax Receipts

Government Tax Receipts

Tax Receipts pay for the Goods and Services the Government provides us but none of us likes to pay Taxes. How then do we expect the Government to pay the bills, if it does not want to print money to do so? To pay its bills, the Government imposes and collects Taxes from all American Citizens and Businesses. These Tax Receipts are the Government Revenues, which are broken down as shown below for Fiscal Year 2011.

The roughly $2.3 Trillion Tax Receipts for Fiscal Year 2011 are derived as follows: 34% from personal Income Tax, 20% from Payroll Tax, 13% from Corporate Income Tax, 24% from Ad-Valorem Tax and 6% from fees and charges.

Despite the well-itemized Tax Receipts, the Government has no solid framework or principle on how to impose and collect Taxes from American Citizens and Businesses. It just trudges along.

The point I am driving home is this. The Federal Government imposes and collects Taxes from individual American citizens and businesses. Congress sets the tax rates ---- meaning it has the power to raise or lower the tax rates of all Americans. Thus, Congress has total control over the Revenue component, just as it

has over the Expenditure component of the so-called Budget Deficit equation, defined as,

Government Budget Deficit   =   Government Revenue –
Government Expenditure

or

Government Budget Deficit   =   Government Tax Receipts –
Government Expenditure

If the US Congress has total control over the two components of the so-called Government Budget Deficit, what then is the Government's problem reducing the Budget Deficit or even balancing the Budget? All it has to do is increase taxes high enough to obtain the Revenue it wants, to match its expected Expenditure. It's as simple as that.

Furthermore, Congress gave authority to the Federal Reserve and Treasury Department to print sufficient money into circulation in the American economy. As such, Congress also has some Power over how much money should be printed into circulation in the American Economy. It makes the Laws.

Thus, why does the Government not print enough money to reduce the Budget Deficit or balance the Budget and National Debt? There will be no inflation because the amount of money presently in circulation in the hands of Consumers is much less than the Real Wealth of goods and services we have already produced. This shortfall in real money supply, the real deficit, is why we have so many foreclosures, unsold homes, cars and other goods and services. There is no money in the hands of consumers to buy these goods and services already on our shelves and hence, they go to waste, while we waste human lives.

Just to demonstrate how ridiculous and silly this Budget Deficit issue is, let's visualize the following scenario. Let's imagine that the whole West Coast of the United States has been destroyed by a massive Earthquake, the whole East coast by enormous Tsunami and Flood, the whole South by a humongous Hurricane, and the whole Midwest by gargantuan Tornadoes, all happening simultaneously. The destruction is total and so massive that there is hunger and starvation all over America.

Furthermore, let's assume that most of the businesses have been destroyed, resulting in mass poverty and huge unemployment. As a result, the United States has no Tax Receipts from businesses and individual citizens but now has to spend trillions of dollars to rebuild the infrastructure and help the surviving Americans have a life ---- zero Tax Receipts and trillions of dollars in Expenditure. We now have a monumental Government Budget Deficit.

According to the Budget Deficit Hawks and Charlatans, we must reduce Government spending or balance the Government Budget, even under such a scenario. What should the Government do? Wait until it collects enough taxes to match the anticipated Expenditure before saving the few American lives left from the destruction or do nothing and let the few survivors die away.

This hypothetical scenario just shows how ludicrous and stupid this whole Government Budget Deficit issue is. It just makes no sense. We seem to value money more than life.

The Government Budget Deficit and National Debt are nothing but money, an IOU or mere symbol for the exchange of real wealth of goods and services. By not helping the American citizens in dire straits, we value money more than life. This is the situation today, as American citizens are rendered homeless through foreclosures, while weeds and junk take over empty homes in blighted neighborhoods. Hundreds of thousands or possibly a few million empty homes and millions of homeless

We are Destroying the American Economy and Ourselves

Americans in the midst of tremendous abundance. All in the name of Money, a mere coupon, deliberately made scarce and more important than American lives.

These aside, let's take a closer look at the Government Tax collection process. The annual budget is usually passed before Taxes are collected and hence, Congress has no idea how much Tax it will collect to match its Expenditure for the Fiscal Year. This means Congress is trying to balance projected Tax Receipts with its budgeted Expenditure. How can this be? If this is not voodoo economics, what is? Even Houdini will chuckle at this money (Budget) balancing illusion by the Unites States Congress.

This is what the so-called Government Budget Deficit is all about --- reducing an illusion of an illusion. Houdini, where are you? The budget deficit is an illusion and so is money, phantom wealth that has no intrinsic value except at the point of transaction. To crown it all, the Tax Receipts for the budgeting process is also vaporware, an engineering lingo for non-existent stuff, at the time of budgeting.

All what Congress is doing is really balancing money with money, a mere accounting chit. Even then, this money-based Government Budget Deficit is not the Nation's Budget Deficit. For the Government is not the Nation.

CHAPTER FOUR

THE GOVERNMENT IS NOT THE NATION

It is very easy for us to assume that the Government is the Nation, especially when we hear the common mantra, Government of the people by the people for the people. Furthermore, observing the absolute powers and authority exercised by the Governments of Dictators like Saddam Hussein and Muammar Gaddafi in Iraq and Libya respectively, it appears that the Government is the Nation. Both Democratic Governments as in the United States and the Dictatorships as in Iraq and Libya seem to be above the citizens, who have the sovereign power of the Nation.

Only when both Saddam Hussein and Muammar Gaddafi were fished out from their rat holes and executed did it dawn on the citizens of Iraq and Libya, and many in the world that the Government is not the Nation. The Government of Saddam Hussein and Muammar Gaddafi are gone but the Nations of Iraq and Libya still stand. Similarly, the Government of President George W. Bush is gone but the Nation, United States, still stands albeit under the government of another President, Barack Obama.

In modern Political Democracies like the United States, the Government is a creation of the citizenry through one person one vote. The Government exists only to serve the citizenry and not to subjugate them. Only the citizens are sovereign and they are the Nation.

Governments come and go but the Nation still stands because the Government is not the Nation. So, what exactly is a Government and what is a Nation?

What is a Government?

A Government is the governing body of a Nation, State or Community. The word "government" is derived from the Latin word "gubanare" meaning to govern or manage. Government is a creation of the citizenry to serve them, not subjugate them; for sovereignty belongs to the people of the Nation.

What is a Nation?

A Nation Is a large aggregate of people united by common descent, culture, language or history, inhabiting a specific territory.

Thus, a Nation or State is the ultimate social institution of any society, while the Government is a component social institution of the Nation, as are Households and Businesses. Hence, as previously described, we can comfortably state that a Nation includes a Government, Households and Businesses. And in mathematical terms we can show the following.

Nation = **Households + Businesses + Government**

Nation's Budget = **Households' Budgets + Businesses' Budgets + Government Budget**

Nation's Budget Deficit = **Households' Budget Deficits + Businesses' Budget Deficits + Government Budget Deficit**

Once more, we can easily discern that a Nation's Budget is made up of the Budgets of Households, Businesses and Government. Furthermore, the Nation's Budget Deficit is made up of the Budget Deficits of Households, Businesses and Government.

The question then is, why is the Government Budget Deficit equated to the Nation's Budget Deficit? Who made such an assumption and why? When did the Government become the Nation? These are questions Economists and Deficit Hawks touting Government Budget Deficit as the Nation's Budget Deficit must answer.

Even going further, we may pose the following questions:

When and how did the following theories come about?

That,

Government Revenue = Nation's Revenue

Government Expenditure = Nation's Expenditure

And since **Budget Deficit = Revenue – Expenditure,** where Revenue is less than Expenditure, the above two equations conclude that

Government Budget Deficit = Nation's Budget Deficit

There is no Financial or Economic theory in the world that stipulates the above or can even make such assumptions, since the Government is not the Nation. The Government is simply a component institution of the Nation.

We can thus, emphatically state that Government Budget Deficit is not the Nation's Budget Deficit. Why then, are we destroying the economy and lives of every human being on this earth with such a spurious or even fraudulent formula?

The most dangerous assumption we humans have made is that **Government is the Nation** and in the process, we created the deadliest formula on earth, destroying the economy of every single nation in this world, including that of the United States.

CHAPTER FIVE

The Deadliest Formula in the World

I always thought Albert Einstein's equation, $E = MC^2$, somehow related to the creation of the Atomic Bomb was the deadliest Formula in the World, until recently.

Seeing the recent riots in Greece because of its collapsing economy and collapsing economies of many European Countries and even the United States, I started looking for a common denominator. My intensive four-year research brought me to the common denominator and simple Formula,

Government Revenue = Government Expenditure

This is the deadliest Formula in the world today, destroying the economy of every single Nation on Earth.

This Formula is the genesis of the Government Budge Deficit, defined as,

Government Budget Deficit   =   Government Revenue –
Government Expenditure

where, Government Expenditure is greater than Government Revenue.

This simple, innocent looking Formula is what is presently decimating the economies of Greece, Portugal, Iceland, Ireland, Spain, Italy and many other countries of the world, including the economy of the United States.

The questions any reasonable person would ask are these:

1. Who invented this Formula?

Government Budget Deficit = Government Revenue –
Government Expenditure

where Government Expenditure is greater than Government Revenue

2. Why is this Budget Deficit Formula applied to Governments that do not manufacture any products or produce any services that generate revenues like private businesses, or earn incomes from jobs like households? Rather, Governments obtain their revenues through the appropriation of portions of households' incomes and revenues of businesses by the imposition of taxes. Are mandatory taxes actual revenues?

3. Why do we use Government Budget Deficit as the gauge or indicator for the economic health of the Nation? After all, the so-called Government Budget Deficit is not even the Nation's Budget Deficit as has been lucidly explained previously.

4. Why does the Government of a Nation with the Authority to print money, not print enough to match its Expenditure, thereby balancing the Government Budget or even the so-called National Debt?

5. Why do we assume that the National Debt is the cumulative annual Government Budget Deficits over the years? In short, what do we mean by National Debt and how do we calculate it?

National Debt

As shown and proven throughout this book, Government is not the Nation. Thus, the cumulative annual Government Budget Deficits over the years is Government Debt and not Nation's Debt. Since the Nation comprises of the core institutions like Government, Businesses and Households, then

Nation's Debt   =   Government Debt + Businesses' Debt + Households' Debt

In other words, National Debt is the total sum of Private Debt and Government or Public Debt. It's that simple and straight forward.

How then did we come to the conclusion that Government or Public Debt is the Nation's Debt, when the Government is not the Nation?

As shown and proven throughout this Volume I and the upcoming Volume II of this book, there is no National Debt, just as there is no National Budget Deficit. The only thing close to a National Debt is the cumulative Trade Deficits resulting from our importing more than we are exporting. Thus, foreign countries like China, Japan, Europe and others use their trade surpluses with the United States, to buy United States Government Instruments like Treasury Bonds. These foreign bond-holdings resulting from the trade surpluses are what we call our National Debt. Is this really a fact? The answer is a resounding no.

Let's assume that China, one of our foreign Bond-holders, buys United States Real Estate with its trade surplus instead of the Government Bonds or even buys US Corporations instead of the Treasury Instruments, would we still claim that the Chinese ownership of US Real Estate or US Corporations is our National Debt? Of course not. It is thus, very silly and ludicrous for us to assume or insinuate that Foreign Bond-holdings resulting from our Trade Deficit is our National Debt. It is not and hence, we have no National Debt.

We now know that Government Debt which is wrongly equated as National Debt is derived from the cumulative annual Government Budget Deficits over the years. The Government Budget Deficit is in turn derived from the formula,

Government Budget Deficit   =   Government Revenue –

where the Government Expenditure is greater than the Government Revenue.

The question we need to pose is this. Why is this Government Budget Deficit Formula used as the gauge for the economic well-being of the Nation instead of the main Accounting Equation of Balance,

Assets = Liabilities + Owner's Equity

This equation is the very foundation of Financial Statements and Double-Entry Bookkeeping in Accounting. Now, the so-called Government Budget Deficit is not part of the Financial Statements and Double-entry Bookkeeping in Economics or Accounting. Rather, Government Revenues and Government Expenditures individually and separately are, and they are respectively placed under Credits and Debits in the Ledger of the Double-entry Bookkeeping System briefly described in the following chapter.

CHAPTER SIX

FINANCIAL STATEMENTS AND DOUBLE-ENTRY BOOKKEEPING

Double-entry bookkeeping is a set of rules in accounting involving simultaneously dual transactions of matching debits and credits. It's main purpose is to check errors, to ensure that the debits always match credits. Any mismatch, discrepancy or gap between the debit and credit indicates an error in financial statements.

There are four main financial statements in Accounting: (1) balance sheets, (2) income statements, (3) cash-flow statements and (4) shareholders' equity statements.

Balance Sheet

This is a Financial Statement that shows what a person, household or any entity for that matter, owns and owes for a specific period of time. It is a document that is divided evenly into two sections, with the left section showing assets (what is owned), and the right section showing liabilities (what is owed) and equity (ownership residual value or interest). It is represented by the formula,

Assets = Liabilities + Owner's Equity

This is the core Accounting Equation or Formula that must always be in balance. It applies to individuals, households, businesses, governments and even nations.

Income Statement

This is also called the profit and loss statement showing how much an entity made and spent over a specific period of time. It gives a snapshot of the Gross Income and Expenses, and profit or loss. It is represented by the following formula,

Profit or Loss = Gross Income – Expenses

Cash-flow Statement

This Financial Statement shows the exchange of money between an entity and the outside world. It gives a snapshot of the entity's inflow and outflow of cash during a certain period of time, and is represented by the following formula,

Net Cash-flow = Cash Inflow – Cash Outflow

Cash-flow is completely distinct from an Income Statement but is extremely important because if an entity does not have cash, it cannot pay its bills and purchase assets.

Shareholders' Equity Statement

This is a Financial Statement that shows changes in interests of the entity's Shareholders over a certain period of time.

Now, all four Financial Statements above are part of the double-entry bookkeeping system and are interrelated. Changes in Revenues and Expenses are immediately reflected in the Balance Sheet. Cash-flow changes also show prominently as cash assets in the Balance Sheet. No single one of these financial statements alone can tell the full story of the financial well-being of an entity but combined, they provide a very vivid and complete picture of the financial health of the entity.

As shown earlier, the budget deficit is derived from Revenues and Expenditures. Since Revenues and Expenditure do not stand alone but are part of the double-entry bookkeeping, where does the so-called budget deficit fit in? How did this budget deficit come to stand alone as the definer of the economic health of a family,

business, government or even nation? Who invented this formula that does not even exist in Accounting? Still seeking answers.

But just like households and businesses, Government Revenues and Government Expenditures must also fit into the core Accounting equation of balance, the Balance Sheet

Government Assets   = Government Liabilities +
Government Equity

Again, the Government is not the Nation and hence, the Government Assets are not the same as the Nation's Assets, and the Government Budget Deficit is also not the Nation's Budget Deficit.

It's now quite obvious that the so called Government Budget Deficit is an illusion, a fraud. So how did the budget deficit hawks and charlatans succeed in convincing most Americans that the Government budget deficit is the Nation's budget deficit, and that the nation is profligate and going broke? Through deceit and lies by first equating the Government Budget to the Nation's Budget and then comparing the Nation's Budget to the Family Budget.

CHAPTER SEVEN

YOUR FAMILY BUDGET IS NOT THE NATION'S BUDGET

The greatest fraud and deceit perpetrated by the Deficit Hawks is to compare the Family Budget or Checkbook to a Nation's Budget or Checkbook. Without hesitation and no valid proof, they emphatically state that, "if my family spends beyond its means like the Government, we would be bankrupt and wretched". "Thus, the Government (not even the Nation) must be as fiscally prudent as the average American family which balances its books". In short, they want the Government (not the Nation) to budget its financial transactions in such a way that its expenditures at least, always match its revenues, so as not to incur a deficit. This they call a balanced budget and hence, the penchant for the balanced budget amendment.

Let's end this deceit and fallacy here and NOW. Your family is not the Government and the Government is not the Nation. Your family does not have an Army, Air-force, Navy and Coast Guard to protect the borders of the United States. Your family does not have a Court or Judicial System that arbitrates disputes between you and your neighbor based on the Constitution, so that you do not kill each other. And most important, your family does not print and circulate money into the United States economy. The Government does, on behalf of the Nation.

Thus, a family's financial transactions including its budget are totally different from a Government's financial transactions including its budget. This is so because families do not print money but the Government of a Nation does. If they (families) did, they would just print money, whenever they want to do their groceries or buy a home or a car.

Instead, a family earns money printed by the Government of the Nation. Hence, its budget is based on the Nation's printed money. As such, the family has to ensure that it does not spend more than it earns. Likewise, businesses use money printed by the Government of the Nation. Hence, they must always check their Revenues against their Expenses for fiscal responsibility.

On the other hand, the Nation, whose citizens have authorized the Government to print money, is not shackled with balancing Revenues and Expenditures. It can always print enough money to match the Nation's Expenditure (not just the Government's Expenditure).

In other words, the Government of the Nation prints and supplies money into the overall economy and hence, its major function is to ensure that the money supply matches the real wealth of goods and services already produced within the country, at all times. But does the Government of the Nation do so? The simple and straight answer is no. The next question is, why not?

The simple answer is ignorance, and this is fully explained in the upcoming Volume II of this book. In the interim, let's continue with our argument that the Nation consists of the Government, Households and Businesses. This means, the

Nation = **Households + Businesses + Government**

Nation's Income = **Households' Incomes + Businesses' Incomes + Government Income**

Nation's Expenditure = **Households' Expenditures + Businesses' Expenditures + Government Expenditure**

To satisfy the double-entry bookkeeping requirements for balancing credits and debits, we can conclude that

Households' incomes = Households' Expenditures

Businesses' Incomes = Businesses' Expenditures

Government Income = Government Expenditure

and

Nation's Income = Nation's Expenditure

This particular equation above is what applies to the Nation as a whole and not the equation,

Government Income = Government Expenditure

For, the Government is not the Nation.

Now, in economics, the Nation's Income is also the Gross Domestic product, GDP, which is the total monetary value of all final goods and services produced within a country's borders in a year.

This is so because, as the nation's goods and services flow out from the producing companies, the Gross Domestic Product becomes the Gross National Income. In short, the Gross Domestic Product (GDP) and Gross National Income (GNI) must always be equal or,

GDP = GNI

Let's shorten these labels by taking out the Gross and hence,

DP = NI

or,

Domestic Product = Nation's Income

Furthermore, GDP is defined in economics by the following Formula,

$$GDP = C + G + I + NX$$

where:

"**C**" is all private consumption or Consumer Spending in a Nation's economy

"**G**" is Total Government Spending

"**I**" is Total investment Spending by all Businesses within the Nation

"**NX**" is the Nation's Total Net Exports, calculated as Total Exports minus Total Imports or NX = Total Exports – Total Imports.

In other words, GDP is the Total Spending or Total Expenditure by Consumers, Businesses and Government, plus the Nation's Expenditure on Imports less Foreigners Expenditure on our Exports. Thus, GDP also equals a Nation's Total Expenditure, i.e.

Gross Domestic Product = Nation's Expenditure

Now, we have earlier on shown that Gross Domestic Product or Domestic Product equals the Nation's Income. As such,

GDP = Nation's Income = Nation's Expenditure

We have come full circle, back to our earlier conclusion that

Nation's Income = Nation's Expenditure

__and not,__

Government Income = Nation's Income

Government Expenditure = Nation's Expenditure

The equation

Nation's Income = Nation's Expenditure

can stand alone, on its own, without being part of the double-entry bookkeeping system in Accounting. This equation will be described in more detail in Volume II of this book but for now, I will assert that the Real Nation's Deficit is when the Nation's Expenditure is greater than the Nation's Income or

Real Deficit = Nation's Income – Nations Expenditure

where the Nation's Expenditure is greater than the Nation's Income.

This is a fundamental economic principle that all Nations on earth, including the United States must adhere to and not the fallacy,

Nation's Budget Deficit   =   Government Revenue –
Government Expenditure

as in present conventional economics, where the Government Expenditure is greater than the Government Income.

This Equation or Formula

Nation's Budget Deficit   =   Government Revenue –
Government Expenditure

is not simply phony but a monumental fraud that is presently destroying the economy of every single Nation in this World, including that of the United States.

Let us now debunk three major Budget Deficit myths oft repeated in public. The first myth is that,

Families cannot spend more than they earn and neither should the Government

This is patently false. Whenever a family takes a loan to buy a home, car or for education, it is spending more than it earns. What matters most is the purpose of the borrowing and the ability of the family to service the loan from its earnings and/or savings.

Similarly, a Government can spend more than its Tax Receipts. What matters most is what it's spending the money on. And unlike the family, the Government can always print money to pay its bills. It does not even have to borrow. Why does the Government then borrow money to pay its bills instead of printing more money? Simply, stupidity and has nothing to do with inflation or even hyperinflation, as usually feared. This will be covered fully in Volume II.

The second myth is that,

The Government should borrow more money instead of printing more money for Deficit spending, so as not to cause inflation

This is another fallacy. Inflation is not caused by just too much money in an economy. Rather, inflation is caused by too much money pursuing too few goods in an economy. But we do not lack any goods and services in the United States. We have an abundance of virtually everything except the money or cash to buy them.

This means the Government should print more money to match the goods and services we have already produced, the GDP. In other words, inflation will rear its head only when there are no more foreclosed homes, no more homes to buy, no more unsold cars in the auto dealerships, no more computers to buy or in fact, no more goods and services to purchase. Thus, our fear of Demand-Pull Inflation is unfounded because what is lacking or scarce in the economy is money or cash, not goods and services we see everywhere in the Nation.

The third myth is that,

Our cumulative large annual Deficits have created a huge National Debt burden for our grandchildren

This is the greatest lie of all, confusing the public the most. The insinuation that, if the present generation continues running a huge national debt, our grandchildren will bear the burden of repayment is totally false. The situation is this. One group of grandchildren will be paying the debt to another group of grandchildren in the same generation. It's as simple as that. The Nation does not owe any debt to anyone, just one group of citizens owing another group within the Nation.

Now, when the Government incurs a debt, it issues a bond, an obligation to pay back the debt with interest to the bondholder. If the bondholders are US citizens, then the Government is merely transferring money from one group of US Citizens (the non-bondholders) to another group of Citizens (the bondholders).

In other words, the so-called national debt, which is an obligation to future United States Tax Payers is also a source of revenue to the American Citizen-Bondholders or -Creditors. Subsequently, there is no generational transfer of indebtedness from one generation to another. We are simply transferring money from one group of Americans to another group of Americans, within the United States. We are thus, not transferring any debt burden to our grandchildren.

The only exception is the National Debt originating from our cumulative Trade Deficits. In this case, our grandchildren will certainly pay interest to the foreign holders of US bonds like China, and Japan. But are the foreign bond-holdings resulting from our cumulative Trade Deficits our National Debt? The simple answer is no.

If Instead of buying United States Bonds with their trade surpluses with us, these foreign countries buy US Real Estate, US Stocks or even US Corporations, does it then mean that these foreign-owned assets ---- US Real Estate, US Stocks or US Corporations, are now our National Debt? Of course not.

Thus, there is nothing like a National Debt. The United States in its entirety owes nobody, and does not have to borrow any money. All it needs to do is print enough money to match the wealth of goods and services we have already produced.

If there Is no National Debt, there is no National Budget Deficit. Hence, the Formula,

Nation's Budget Deficit = Government Revenue –
Government Expenditure

is as good as useless. And this simple but extremely dangerous equation is the cause of the present Great Recession and all the past global recessions, including the Depression of 1929.

I will now briefly describe the history of the Great Depression of 1929 and subsequent recessions, including the present Great Recession of 2007, caused by the phony Budget Deficits.

History of the Devastating impacts of the Phony Budget Deficits on the United States and the World at Large

The Great Depression of 1929

Most people think the Great Depression of the 1930s was caused by the 1929 collapse of the Stock Market. It wasn't. Rather, the actions of the United States President and Congress after the crash caused the Great Depression. The Federal Reserve in conjunction with Congress and the President, reduced the Money supply by one-third, thereby destroying a third of the Money circulating in the Economy. There was a mismatch between the Money Supply and Real Wealth of already produced goods and services. There wasn't sufficient Money in Circulation in the hands of Consumers to purchase already produced Real Wealth --- goods and services.

Adding insult to injury, President Herbert Hoover proposed and Congress (both Republicans and Democrats) passed the Revenue Act of 1932 because they felt Deficit Reduction was the highest economic priority. This Act set in motion the largest tax increase in the history of the United States. They were trying to reduce the Federal Budget Deficit with the ultimate aim of balancing the Federal Budget. Millions of American lives were devastated, and the struggling, fragile economy collapsed.

Europe and Japan followed the footsteps of the United States and their economies also collapsed --- all in the name of reducing a Phony Government Budget Deficit and National Debt or balancing a Phony Government Budget and National Debt.

The continued severity of the Depression in the US gave Roosevelt a landslide victory in the Presidential election of 1932, sweeping into power a Democratic-controlled Senate and House. But, the United States got out of this Depression because of Marriner Eccles, the leading Economist at the time, who advised FDR to increase the Money Supply by spending more. Hence, FDR's massive Government Programs encompassing public works, unemployment relief, tax reform, farm mortgage refinancing, bank guarantees, and passage of laws on child labor, minimum wage, and old-age pension or social security Insurance.

The fortuitous and timely advice to FDR by the then leading economist, Mariner Eccles is why the Federal Reserve Building in Washington DC is named in his honor.

This massive infusion of capital into the economy through Federal Spending increased the money supply while employing Americans at the same time, leading to the eventual amelioration of the Great Depression until 1937.

1937 - 1938

Now in 1937, the Federal Reserve and Roosevelt Administration made a fundamental error. They felt the Great Depression was over and drastically reduced spending, while tightening monetary policy for fear of inflation. Furthermore, the new Social Security Taxes, which began to be collected in 1936 and 1937, further shrunk the money supply and the economy collapsed. Once again, a mismatch of Money Supply and Real Wealth caused another nasty but avoidable economic plunge. There was insufficient money in circulation in the hands of Consumers to purchase already existing goods and services, to keep revving up the economy.

1973 – 1975 Recession

"This period stood apart from many other U.S. recessions as it was marked distinctly by stagflation – the combination of high unemployment and high inflation. The United States faced a surge in oil prices due to OAPEC's (Organization of Arab Petroleum Exporting Countries) oil embargo, combined with increased spending due to the Vietnam War and a stock market crash after the collapse of the Bretton Woods monetary relation system, officially putting an end to the economic boom which followed WWII. Unemployment peaked at 9% and, although the recession is recognized as having ended in 1975, the country experienced low economic growth for years afterwards".[1]

Once more, there was an imbalance or mismatch in the Money Supply (Money actually circulating in the economy and in the hands of Consumers) and the Real Wealth of already produced goods and services. A lot of money was spent on the Vietnam War and not sufficient money in the hands of Consumers (People and Businesses) to continue purchasing the Real Wealth of goods and services, to keep revving up the economy.

1980 – 1982 Recession

"In the late 1970's, inflation was on the rise in the United States, in part left over from the 1973 recession. As a result, the Federal Reserve tightened monetary policy considerably, in turn causing investment purchases to drop as capital became less available. By winter of 1982, however, inflation continued to drop and unemployment rose for several years".[2]

Again, this recession was actually caused by a mismatch of Money in Circulation (Money actually in the hands of Consumers) and the Real Wealth of goods and services available for purchase. The Fed's tightening of monetary policy in the guise of fighting inflation, reduced the Money Supply in the Economy, causing less

Money available for the purchase of already existing goods and services. This was what created, exacerbated and prolonged the recession.

The Great Recession of 2007

The present Great Recession which began in December 2007 is still flexing its muscle as more millions of people lose their homes, jobs and assets, on top of the earlier millions. A problem that started in the United States has become a global phenomenon, devastating lives all over the world.

This Great Recession of 2007 appears to be the worst since the Great Depression of 1929. An American Economy built on a shaky foundation of Financial Sand --- overpriced stock market, overvalued homes, heavily indebted Consumers and risky, fraudulent mortgages --- finally collapsed, dragging along the investment bank Bear Stearns and several major American institutions like AIG, Lehman Brothers, GM, Merrill Lynch, Countrywide, to name a few. Some of these Institutions were bailed out by the Federal Government, while others were allowed to go under or be bought by financially stronger Institutions. Unemployment has continued unabated, while home losses are getting out of control with millions of homes underwater.

This current Recession was not caused by the stock market collapse or the housing bubble bust. It was caused by a mismatch of the Money in Circulation (Money actually in the hands of Consumers --- People and Businesses) and the Real Wealth of goods and services already available for purchase. Consumers were and still are heavily indebted, and hence, there is no purchasing power.

Yes, the Federal Reserve and Federal Government poured a lot of money into the Economy to increase the Money Supply, but the Money was in the wrong hands ---- Banks, Financial Institutions and other big Corporations, not in the hands of Real Consumers who actually buy the Real Wealth of goods and services to rev up the Economy. In short, the Federal Reserve's Quantitative Easings, QE1 and QE2, to stimulate the economy, were trapped in Wall Street and the money was mostly used for speculation. Most of this money never reached Main Street or the Real Economy.

For any Economy to be healthy, the simple but profound principle of Money in Circulation in the hands of Real Consumers matching Real Wealth of goods and services already in the market must always hold. Expressing it in mathematical form,

Money in Circulation in the hands of Consumers = Real Wealth of goods and services.

Unless, this simple but fundamental balancing principle is adhered to, the present Great Recession will continue, foreclosures will accelerate, unemployment will keep rising and the economy will not see the light at the end of the tunnel. The present shortfall in Real Money Supply compared to Real Wealth is what we call the Real Deficit.

In other words, the **Real Deficit** is the difference between Real Wealth and Money in Circulation in the hands of Real Consumers, where the Real Wealth is greater than Money in Circulation or,

Real Deficit = Real Wealth > Money in Circulation in the hands of Real Consumers

and not the **Phony Budge Deficit,** defined as Government Expenditure greater than Government Income (Government Tax Receipts) or,

Phony Budget Deficit   =   Government Expenditure >
Government Tax Receipts

The greatest enemies of the present Great Recession of 2007 are those espousing reduction of this useless, senseless, meaningless and monumentally stupid **Phony Government Budget Deficit.** A simple but extremely dangerous idea that is destroying economies all over the world, especially the Economy of the United States.

Just as in 1932 and 1937, the present attempt by Democrats and Republicans to reduce the **Phony Government Budget Deficit** or the cumulative Budget Deficits called National Debt in the interim by as much as $1.5 trillion will only plunge the current, fragile and recessionary Economy into greater depths. And reducing the so-called National Debt by about $4 to 6 Trillion within 10 years, as propounded by Rep. Paul Ryan and the Deficit Hawks, will totally decimate the U.S Economy. This is stupidity and foolhardiness of the highest order that borders on insanity.

Just as the monumentally stupid idea of "Phlebotomy" or "Bloodletting" destroyed hundreds of millions of lives, throughout the world for several thousand years, including that of the first President of the United States, George Washington, it appears this extremely silly idea of reducing the **Phony Government Budget Deficit** or balancing the **Phony Government Budget** is also going to destroy millions of lives while laying waste, economies of the world, from one country to another.

It seems we human beings do not learn or learn too late. A very dangerous habit! How different life would be in the United States, without this phony Government Budget Deficit.

CHAPTER NINE

What will the United States be like if this phony Government Budget Deficit Achilles Hill is removed from our American Psyche?

The following are the headlines in the News Media as States and Local Governments go broke because of Budget Deficits.

"Governors brace for inevitable cuts to states as debt debate rages on

'No matter what happens, states are going to get less money from the federal government,' Miss. governor says".

"Debt ceiling uncertainty puts states at risk

'We all fear and see the specter, the dark clouds that would hide our beautiful blue skies and mountains,' Salt Lake City's mayor says".

"States may hit borrow button if federal aid cut".

"Strapped states cutting unemployment benefits".

'Unprecedented' moves even as joblessness stays high, new report says".

"City officials struggling to make ends meet".

"9 American cities going broke".

"Alabama County files biggest municipal bankruptcy".

These are the consequences of the phony Federal Budget Deficits.

Without this belief and fear of the Budget Deficit, we would create an enthralling and magnificently visionary future for all Americans and the World.

Without this Budget Deficit fear, the constant fight between Democrats and Republicans, Fiscal Conservatives and Keynesians will be history. For, we will always have all the money we need to do whatever we want, while not overburdening ourselves with excessive taxation --- a win-win situation for all.

Without this Budget Deficit issue,

1. We will increase social spending on entitlements like Social Security, Unemployment Compensation, Medicare, Medicaid and Welfare Payments.

2. We will have Universal Health Insurance for every American, for Health is Wealth.

3. We will ensure that every single American has the basics of life --- food, shelter and clothing. No more homeless Americans. No more hungry Americans, especially children and single mothers. No more poor and wretched Americans.

4. We will continuously rebuild our broken and dilapidated infrastructure, and even build new ones --- roads, bridges, dams, levees, sewer systems, airports, seaports, schools and parks, while employing millions of Americans in high paying jobs.

5. We will expand our telecommunication system to every nook and cranny in America, and make the ubiquitous Internet (wireless and wired broadband) available to every American, any and every where in the United States.

6. We will upgrade our electric grid and in fact, deploy the most technologically advanced and most efficient smart grids in every community in every section of the United States.

7. We will usher into the United States, the most sophisticated and most technologically advanced mass transportation system in the World, integrating air, sea and land transport into a cohesively efficient whole. This will of course include the fastest and most efficient bullet trains.

8. We will accelerate the deployment of the latest technologies in renewable energy systems to replace carbon-emitting fossil fuel, while leading the world in Research and Development in this area.

9. We will restore our dying forests, vanishing fresh water, fisheries, coral reefs, topsoil, and biodiversity back to life, while stabilizing our climate with massive reduction in carbon emission.

10. We will transform our Education System into a 21st Century marvel --- the best of the best in the world --- where the cream of the crop from our educational institutions become Teachers, who are very highly paid. Our Schools and students will continue to set the standards for global excellence

11. We will expand and modernize a well-funded NASA to lead the world in Space Exploration, Research and Development.

12. We will expand Research and Development in every sphere of life ---- Science, Technology, Manufacturing, Government, Arts and Education itself, thereby creating a conducive environment for all Americans, especially our scholars and entrepreneurs to unleash their creativity ---- thereby bringing to fruition, the most innovative inventions and products that would make life easier for humanity.

13. We will .... add your own great ideas, because we are no longer constrained by the phony Government Budget Deficit.

As you can see, the Government Budget Deficit is all about money, nothing more. With more money, which means bigger Government Budget Deficits, we can do a lot more and live a better life. Hence, why are we afraid of bigger Government Budget Deficits? In short, why are we afraid of more money in our lives to live better lives? And what exactly is money ?

CHAPTER TEN

WHAT EXACTLY IS MONEY AND WHAT IS REAL WEALTH?

Our quest or penchant for money reminds us of the well-known story of King Midas and his golden touch. With the exception of his daughter, Marygold, King Midas loved and was only happy to be around gold. He simply loved gold, the currency at the time, just like money today. He spent most of his time in the underground cell or dungeon, playing with his gold. That was his happiness ---- Gold.

Then one day, a stranger visited Midas in his cell and Midas instantly knew that this was a god because of his radiance. It was Dionysus, the god of life, who soon found out that Midas was not satisfied with the gold he had. He wanted more gold than any other human being in the World.

Sensing the unhappiness of Midas, Dionysus asks him what would make him happy. Midas replied that he wanted the golden touch and that would make him the happiest man in the world. The god then granted Midas' wish.

From then on anything Midas touched turned into gold. He was very excited and in his happiness, he took a glass of water to drink only to see it turn into gold. His food tuned into gold in his mouth. Midas was now literally starving and it was when he kissed his daughter and she turned into gold that he realized that the gift of the golden touch was a curse.

Now very miserable, Midas sought the god, Dionysus to reverse the gift of the golden touch because he now hated gold for all its worth. Dionysus obliges and tells Midas to wash himself in the Pactolus River and sprinkle the river water on anything he had previously touched into gold. Midas obeyed the god's instructions and everything he sprinkled the river water came back to normal including his daughter, Marygold.

The story ends with Midas playing with his grandchildren many years later but with consummate hatred for gold. He now realized that gold was not real wealth. Food, water, his family and the basic things in life we take for granted were the real wealth.

This Greek mythology is still relevant today, where most humans still think that money is real wealth. Is it real wealth? If not, what exactly is money?

What Exactly is Money?

Money is only a convenient transactional instrument for the exchange of real wealth ----- our labor, ideas, land, inventions, oil and gas, health care, food and other goods and services that are useful to humanity. Money in itself has no intrinsic value.

It is an illusory wealth that most people have mistakenly accepted as real wealth. That's a fallacy. Money never was, never has been and never will be real wealth. Rather, it is a mere symbol for the exchange of real wealth. It is also a symbol of the economic health of a nation.

Just as freely circulating blood produces health in a person, freely circulating money in one's life, gives one economic health. As such, like blood clot, hoarding money by hiding it under the mattress or in some special savings Account out of fear, stops the free flow of money, resulting in economic sickness. Similarly, when a nation's money is being hoarded or monopolized by the wealthy, financial institutions like banks and corporations, it does not circulate freely and the nation becomes economically sick.

This is the present cause of the Great Recession of 2007. There isn't enough money in the hands of Consumers circulating in the economy to buy up the real wealth of goods and services we have already produced.

What exactly is Money Supply or Circulation of Money in the hands of Consumers?

This is a very important question. The Money Supply or circulation of money we are talking about is actual cash, money or liquid financial instruments immediately accessible and available to Consumers (People and Organizations), to purchase available goods and services in the Real or Main Street Economy, where goods and services are produced, bought and sold. It is quite distinct from money hoarded by financial institutions like banks and corporations, and hence, not in circulation in the Real Economy.

It is also quite different from Wall Street speculative money, operating outside Main Street Economy. Such funds flow from banks and other financial institutions into speculation on Wall Street and other gambling establishments, and are recycled back into the banks and financial institutions without touching the Real Economy, thereby creating Wall-Street money-circulation traps outside Main Street Economy.

These Wall Street money-circulation traps are why all the trillions of dollars poured into the United States Economy (Main Street and Wall Street) by the Government and Federal Reserve seem ineffective in ameliorating the Great Recession of 2007. Most of such money continue circulating from banks and other financial institutions to Wall Street and back to the financial institutions. Very little or none of such funds go into the Real Economy, where the Great Recession is biting hard.

In the heat of the present Great Recession, the Federal Reserve bought a lot of Treasury securities (Bills, Bonds and Notes) in the open market. With this purchase, the Fed had more securities, while the previous owners who sold the securities to the Fed, now have more cash to lend or spend, to revive the Real Economy. Unfortunately, these new cash owners -- Banks, Corporations and Wealthy Elites -- are not lending or spending the new cash in the Real Economy but are hoarding and using it to speculate on Wall Street, to make more money with money. Thus, the Fed's "open market" operations expected to spur economic activity in the Real Economy, is continuously boosting speculation on Wall Street.

Subsequently, the Great Recession of 2007 continues and may turn into the Great Depression of the 21st Century, unless sufficient money is made available to Consumers, that matches the real wealth of goods and services (GDP) already on our shelves.

But most important of all, we must never forget that food, shelter and clothing came into existence before money, a mere coupon, a convenient transactional instrument for the exchange of real wealth of goods and services. We human beings, especially Americans cannot do without food, shelter and clothing but we can do without money.

Hence, our present focus on budgets, budget deficits and even GDP, all pertaining to only money, is misplaced. We should rather focus on life and the well-being of every American ---- in fact, every human being on this earth, while using money as a convenient tool for the exchange of real wealth.

What Exactly is Real Wealth?

Real Wealth is Life itself, and the Quality of Life is the real measure of Real Wealth. Money is not Real Wealth but simply a symbolic tool, an IOU for the exchange of Real Wealth. We buy some of the Real Wealth with Money but others are simply priceless and cannot be bought with Money. We cannot buy Love, Happiness, Laughter and Clean Air with Money.

In other words, Real Wealth includes clean air, clean water, fertile soil, healthy food, caring relationships, loving parents, great family, wonderful children, peaceful communities, safe and clean neighborhoods, freedom, knowledge, creativity, good education, good health, fulfilling opportunities for service, artistic leisure, love, happiness, meditation, spirituality and a sustainable ecosystem of the Earth which holds all wealth in its bosom. Most of these are not included in the GDP (the total US Economy).

Furthermore, helpful technologies and environmentally-sensitive businesses, infrastructure like good roads, bridges, schools, non-polluting power plants, homes, and helpful manufactured goods like cars, airplanes, TVs, Computers, Software and life enhancing services are also Real Wealth. Some of these are what comprise the US GDP of roughly $14.93 Trillion for 2011.

Besides the phantom wealth called Money and the Real Wealth just described, we also have phony Government Budget Deficit and Real Nation's Deficit described and differentiated explicitly below.

Phony Budget Deficit and Real Deficit

Presently, the Federal Budget Deficit is defined as the Difference between the Government-authorized Budget or Government Expenditure and Government Tax Receipts, where the Budgeted Amount (Expenditure) is greater than expected Tax Receipts. This is the **Phony Federal Budget Deficit** and makes no sense. In other words,

Phony Budget Deficit = Government-authorized Budgeted Amount > Government Tax Receipts

$$= \text{Government Expenditure} >$$
$$\text{Government Tax Receipts}$$

The **Real Deficit,** on the other hand, is the shortfall in the Real Money Supply, vis-à-vis the Real Wealth. In short, **Real Deficit** is the difference between Real Wealth and the Money in Circulation in the hands of Consumers or Consumer's Purchasing Power, where the Money in Circulation or Consumer's Purchasing Power is less than the Real Wealth.

Hence,

Real Deficit = **Real Wealth > Money in Circulation in the hands of Consumers**

= **Real Wealth > Consumer's Purchasing Power**

This is the Real Deficit all Nations should be concerned about, not the phony Government Budget Deficit --- a mere spurious number.

Now, since the **National Debt** is assumed to be the cumulative annual **Phony Government Budget Deficits** over the years, there is actually no **National Debt**. Hence, this **National Debt** is also phony. The Federal Government prints money and hence, can always print enough money to match the Real Wealth. And this will not cause any inflation.

As previously stated, the so-called debt owed Foreigners by the United States is a trade deficit, nothing more. These cumulative Trade Deficits are not National Debt either, for the foreign holders of US Bonds could have as well used their cumulative Trade Surpluses against us, to buy Unites States Real Estate or US Corporations. If such foreign-owned US Real Estate or US

Corporations are not American National Debt, then the foreign-owned US Treasury Bonds are also not our National Debt.

Having differentiated the phony Government Budget deficit from the Real National Deficit and debunked the myth of the existence of a National Debt, we can now focus on the rapid recovery of the U.S. economy.

For a quick and robust recovery, the US government must ensure that the amount of **Money Circulating** in the Real United States Economy (in the hands of Consumers ---- People and Businesses at least match the **GDP** of roughly **$14.93 Trillion**, i.e.

GDP = Real Wealth = Money in Circulation = $14.93 Trillion.

The **Real Deficit** is when **Real Wealth** of goods and services is greater than the amount of **Money in Circulation in the hands of Consumers**.

Let's assume the **Money in Circulation** (in the hands of Consumers ---- People and Businesses) is **$12 Trillion** in 2011. Then the

Real Deficit	**=**	**Real Wealth – Money in Circulation in the hands of Consumers**
	=	**GDP – Money in Circulation in the hands of Consumers**
	=	**$14.93 Trillion - $12 Trillion = $2.93 Trillion**

On the other hand, let's assume the Government budgeted **$3.60 Trillion** for Expenditures, with projected Tax Receipts of **$2.30 Trillion** for 2011.

Then, the

Phony Budget Deficit   =   Government Expenditure –

Government Tax Receipts

= $3.60 Trillion - $2.30 Trillion = $1.30 Trillion

The above $1.30 Trillion Phony Budget Deficit for 2011 is meaningless, useless and has no relevance in the overall U.S. Economy. But reducing this $1.30 Trillion Phony Budget Deficit, or eliminating (balancing) the $3.60 Trillion Budget entails massive spending cuts and/or huge tax increases. These large spending cuts and/or huge tax increases to cure this Phony Budget Deficit are the cause of the massive unemployment, accelerated home foreclosures, and grim recession, all of which may ultimately destroy the fragile US Economy.

The most important number in the above scenario for 2011 is the **Real Deficit** of **$2.93 Trillion.** The Government, Fed, and Banks must add **$2.93 Trillion** into the overall U.S. Economy (through the hands of Consumers --- People and Businesses) to match the already produced Wealth of goods and services. This balancing act will then prevent real contraction of the economy, with its attendant failing companies, massive unemployment, more foreclosures and prolongation of the Great Recession, as is the case today.

Let's take a more concrete example of the phony Government Budget Deficit and Real National Deficit using Vanuatu Republic as an example

Republic of Vanuatu

Vanuatu, a 'Y' shaped archipelago of 83 islands has a population of roughly 234,000. It is located about 1,085 miles east of

Australia, with Fiji on its east, New Caledonia on the south, and the Solomon Islands on northwest.

It is a fairly large producer of Bananas in the world. Let's assume Vanuatu Private Farmers produce 1 million pounds of Bananas yearly and each pound of Bananas costs $0.50. This means, Vanuatu Farmers will generate $0.50 per pound x 1 million pounds or $500,000 revenue annually. Let's also assume that these Farmers make a profit of 50% and pay 30% tax. Furthermore, let's assume that the Vanuatu Government has budgeted $100,000 per year as the cost of running their Government.

Now, we have two scenarios.

1. Assuming the amount of money in circulation in the hands of Consumers in the Vanuatu economy is $500,000. This means that these Vanuatu Consumers have enough money to buy up all the Bananas for the year. The Vanuatu Farmers profit is $500,000 x 50% = $250,000. The Government tax receipt is 30% x $250,000 = $75,000. The so-called Budget Deficit is Tax Receipt – Government Expenditure = $75,000 - $100,000 = -$25,000.

2. Assuming the amount of money in circulation in the hands of Consumers in the Vanuatu economy is $250,000, these Vanuatu Consumers now do not have enough money to buy up all the Bananas for the year. This means the Vanuatu Farmers will only sell 0.50 million or 500,000 pounds of Bananas costing $250,000, the maximum amount of money the Consumers have in their hands. The Vanuatu Farmers profit is $250,000 x 50% = $125,000. The Government tax receipt is 30% x $125,000 = $37,500. The so-called Budget Deficit is Tax Receipt – Government Expenditure = $37,500 - $100,000 = -$62,500.

As described earlier, the True Vanuatu Nation's Deficit is the shortage of funds in the hands of Vanuatu Consumers ($250,000) to buy all 1 million pounds of Bananas costing $500,000 from the Vanuatu Farmers, as in scenario 2 above.

In other words, the Real Deficit is $500,000 - $250,000 = $250,000, as in scenario 2. There is no Real Deficit in scenario 1 because the real wealth of goods produced (1 million pounds of Bananas costing $500,000) exactly matches the money in circulation in the hands of Consumers in Vanuatu, $500,000.

The so-called Budget Deficits in the above two scenarios, $25,000 in scenario 1 and $62,500 in scenario 2 are phony Budget Deficits, which are not only meaningless but actually useless in the totality of the Vanuatu Economy.

This phony Budget Deficit is what is continuously destroying the economies of countries all over the world, from Spain to Portugal to Ireland to Greece to the United State, and more.

Once again, as mentioned earlier, one of the most important economics guiding principles is the principle of balancing Real Money Supply and Real Wealth. We must never forget that the money in circulation in the hands of Consumers must always match the real wealth of goods and services, for any economy to thrive.

As you can observe in the second scenario for Vanuatu, 500,000 pounds of bananas will go to waste because the country refused to provide sufficient money to its citizens to buy up the real wealth they had already produced. The country valued money more than the real wealth of bananas that the Vanuatu farmers spent their time and life energy to produce.

The bottom line is this. We must always match the Real Money Supply to the Real Wealth of the Nation for the economy to survive and then thrive. In other words,

Money in Circulation in = **Real Wealth of goods**
the hands of Consumers   **and services.**

This specific economic principle of balance and others, essential for a robust economy of any Nation, are succinctly described in the following chapter.

CHAPTER ELEVEN

BRIGHT HARRY'S ECONOMICS PRINCIPLES OF BALANCE

These Principles are described in more details in the upcoming Volume II of this book, but they are summarized here for your convenience. And here they are:

1. The Balancing Principle of Money only

a   **Household Income**   =   **Household Expenditure**

b   **Business Income**   =   **Business Expenditure**

c   **Government Income**   =   **Government Expenditure**

d   **Nation's Income**   =   **Nation's Expenditure**

The above principle involves only balancing money with money. And as you can see in each of the above Formulas, we are simply balancing money with money, nothing more. Each component of each Equation above is an input to either the credit side or debit side of the Double-Entry Bookkeeping System in Accounting. Each of the incomes on the left goes to the Credit side of the ledger and each of the Expenditures on the right goes to the Debit side.

Now, a Double-Entry Bookkeeping System is a set of rules in Accounting for recording financial transactions, where each transaction involves two opposing but equal inputs --- debit and credit. Each transaction is entered twice, one on the debit side and the other on the credit side, as shown above for income and expenditure.

The main purpose of this Double-Entry transaction is to check errors, thereby ensuring that the total debits always equal the total credits.

This means that Formulas 1a, 1b and 1c cannot stand on their own. As such, each component of each Formula is incorporated into either the debit or credit side of the fundamental Accounting Equation of Balance, the Balance Sheet;

Assets = Liabilities + Owner's Equity

This is the most fundamental Formula in Accounting, Economics or Business that gives the true economic well-being or rather the true financial health of any entity. Similarly, Formula 1d which can also stand on its own, as will be fully explained throughout this Volume and in the upcoming Volume II, also gives the true economic health of any entity. It is also a very important Formula and Balancing Principle that can make or break a Nation.

On the other hand, the following Formula being used throughout the world, as the gauge of a Nations' economic health,

National Budget Deficit = Government Tax Receipts – Government Expenditures

where Government Expenditures are greater than Government Tax Receipts, is not only massively fraudulent but very deadly and destroying the economies of Greece, Spain, Portugal, Italy and many others including the United States.

2. The Balancing Principle of Real Money Supply and Real Wealth

Real Money Supply = Real Wealth

where Real Money Supply is the actual amount of money in circulation in the hands of Consumers. Here, we are balancing money with real goods and services we produce. It is unlike the previous Formulas, where money is balanced against money. This is the Formula that matters to Nations.

3. The Balancing Principle of Real Total Spending and Real Wealth

Real Total Spending = Real Wealth

Here also, we are balancing Total amount of Real Spending money with real goods and services we produce. Real Spending on Main Street or the Real Economy is quite distinct from speculating on Wall Street or spending in Gambling Casinos. It is also quite different from Banks and financial Institutions moving money among themselves, without a single cent reaching Main Street.

4. The Optimum Balancing Principle or Equilibrium of Real Money Supply, Real Total Spending and Real Wealth.

Real Money Supply = Real Total spending = Real Wealth

In this case, we simply combined Equations 2 and 3 but we are still balancing money and the real wealth of goods and services we produce, not just balancing money with money. This is the most important equation of all the Balancing Principles, for the economic viability of any Nation. Break this last Principle and your Nation's Economy collapses, as is happening in Greece, Portugal, Spain, Italy and the United States, today.

Formulas 1d and 4 are one and the same as would be shown in the upcoming Volume II of this book. They are the most important equations of economic balance for any nation's economy. They are the gauge for the health of any economy, and can make or break the economy of every single Nation on Earth.

What Formulas 1d and 4 are telling us is that at Equilibrium GDP, when and where aggregate demand intersects aggregate supply, the Real Money Supply must always match the Real Total Spending, which in turn must always match the Real Wealth of goods and services.

This Real Total Spending that matches the Real Wealth is the combined Expenditure of the Government, all Households and all Businesses within the Nation that make up the Social Institutions of the Nation. These core social Institutions and many others are briefly described in the next chapter.

CHAPTER TWELVE

INSTITUTIONS

A Social Institution is a social structure characterized by the cultural norms, language, behavioral patterns, beliefs, regulations and laws of the particular society. All Social Institutions ---- Household or Family, Business, Economics, Law, Government or Politics and Religion, mutually reinforce each other in a cohesive whole.

In a society, where Social Institutions are based on a Top-down model, Political, Economic and Cultural Power are highly concentrated in the hands of the few at the Top. Such Trickle-Down Institutions will ensure that government policies, business regulations, legal systems and even the news media are concentrated and controlled by the few at the Top. This is the Institutional model for most countries of the world, including the United States, where the Top-Down Economic Feudalism and Economic Plutocracy reign supreme.

In a Bottom-Up or Networked Institutional Model, Political, Economic and Cultural Power are distributed evenly but not necessarily equally, in an egalitarian fashion, where equal opportunity, transparency, accountability and partnership rule. This social institutional model is where the Revolutionary Democratic Capitalism, described briefly in the next chapter, fits in.

Since this chapter is just a summarized extract from the upcoming Volumes II and III, my focus here will be on Political and Economic Institutions, especially the Government.

The Government is a creation of the citizenry and its purpose is to serve the citizens and not subjugate them. In the American Political Democracy, the citizens are sovereign and they give power to the government through their (citizens') votes, to do their bidding. Thus, the government is just a tool for the people to protect themselves and their property, but that's not the case with the American Government of today. Something is wrong somewhere.

What is wrong with the American Government?

The problem with the present American Government is that it is not as democratic as it should be. Too much political and economic power is concentrated in the hands of the few at the Top. The few wealthy elites and politically well-connected have too much power compared to the masses.

One person one vote which is political democracy does not necessarily translate into a Democratic Government as in the United States. The power of money in the hands of the few compared to the poverty of the many, adversely influences the democratization of the US Government. The many are so frustrated and even angry at the aloofness of the Government to them that they become apathetic, passive and discouraged to even go to the polls to vote. Unfortunately, failing to exercise their voting rights, they abdicate from their sovereign power, thereby unconsciously giving enormous political and economic power to the few Elites, the large Corporations and Lobbyists. With their enormous capital, these few are able to influence the White House and US Congress to the detriment of the many, turning a supposedly Political Democracy into Political Feudalism and/or Political Plutocracy.

This need not be so because sovereign Power belongs to "We the People", not to the wealthy few, the lobbyists or the politically well-connected. We the people must exercise our sovereign right to vote out those who do not dance to our collective music. We have the voting power to force a change in Washington DC and totally democratize America, Politically, Economically and Culturally.

America is not yet a truly democratic society and hence, we must complete the unfinished business of the Founding Fathers. We must make the United States a truly democratic society, where Political, Economic and Cultural Power is shared by all --- distributed evenly among all citizens. There must be transparency, accountability and effective checks and balances by "We the People" on those we voluntarily chose to govern us.

It is not about how big or small the American Government is. It is about how responsible, effective and democratic the Government is. In short, what we want is a good, democratic Government where those we voted into power are accountable to us, not to Lobbyists, Special Interests, Corporations or the Wealthy Elites. And accountability is assured when "We the People" participate effectively in decisions affecting us and can easily remove elected representatives who abuse their power and the mandate we gave them, while still in possession of our capacity to repeal unpopular laws.

All these will be covered in more details in Volumes II and III but for the United States to be a truly democratic society, there must be full-fledged Political Democracy, Economic Democracy and Cultural Democracy, where each and every American citizen has the sovereign right and opportunity to participate effectively in decisions that affect him or her. In other words, we Americans must democratize all our Institutions.

And that is why America must shift from its present destructive Economic Institution of Feudalistic/Plutocratic Capitalism to the

21st century Revolutionary Democratic Capitalism, summarized in the next chapter.

CHAPTER THIRTEEN

REVOLUTIONARY DEMOCRATIC CAPITALISM

Presently, we face enormous political, economic and cultural challenges that go far beyond Budget Deficits, National Debt, Transfer Payments and Unemployment. In fact, our future and our very existence as human beings on this earth are at stake.

We face tremendous threats from global warming with its attendant ocean surge and floods, ocean pollution, chemical contamination, nuclear and toxic waste, biodiversity loss and depletion of our forests, soil, water aquifers, fisheries and the ozone layer. These aside, toxic chemicals in our water, soil and the food we eat are now disrupting our endocrine system, a catastrophic threat to every person on earth.

The combination of all these threats at the same time is a warning to us all humans, especially we privileged Americans, to wake up and smell the coffee. We are destroying the United states economy, our environment and our lives with our present economic model, which we are also exporting to every single country in the World. We must now change this economic model of ours, if we want to survive and give a chance to the next generation of Americans and in fact, the next generation of human beings on earth. Our present economic model of Feudalistic and Plutocratic Capitalism is not working. It has failed us and now placing us all on the verge of extinction.

The 21st century Knowledge-Intensive Economy demands a different Economic model from our present Industrial-era Economic Model. We must quickly transition into the 21st century economic model of Revolutionary Democratic Capitalism, ensconced in Economic Democracy, which is in turn intertwined with its twin, Political Democracy. This is the future.

The mismatch of our present Economic Feudalism and Economic Plutocracy with our Political Democracy is the bane of our present economic quagmire. Economic Feudalism/Plutocracy and Political Democracy are like oil and water. They do not mix and as long as we maintain these two incompatible social systems, we will continue to be in the same political and economic conundrum, with no end in sight. Only Economic Democracy works hand in hand with Political Democracy, and within Economic Democracy is the Revolutionary Democratic Capitalism.

With this 21st Century Revolutionary Democratic Capitalism, we will solve our Social Security problems, mass Unemployment, Healthcare, Welfare, and the phony Government Budget Deficits and National Debt in one fell swoop.

The sheer magnitude and complexity of today's economic quagmire requires a holistic solution, not a piecemeal one. Only this Revolutionary Democratic Capitalistic economic model offers such a holistic solution. All these will be described in detail, lucidly and simply for easy comprehension in the upcoming Volumes II and III. Very fascinating Economic Model.

We Americans must once more lead the world into the 21st Century Knowledge-intensive economy by truly democratizing or re-democratizing all our Institutions.

In other words, we must jettison our present economic model ---- Feudalistic and Plutocratic Capitalism, for our very survival as human beings --- and jump into the robust and Revolutionary Democratic Capitalism.

We must stop practicing Capitalism without Capitalists. We must no longer practice the type of Capitalism where American citizens are without the very capital that makes Capitalism what it is. In other words, we must democratize Capital for all Americans, if we believe in Capitalism and Democracy.

One person one vote pertains to political democracy only. For us to have a truly democratic society, we need the triplet of Political Democracy, Economic Democracy and Cultural Democracy, all interacting simultaneously into a cohesive whole.

Communism and socialism are mere political systems and not economic systems despite what Karl Marx says. There is only one economic system in the world, Capitalism. And there are only three versions of Capitalism --- Feudalistic, Plutocratic and Democratic Capitalism

Communism and Socialism are both Feudalistic and or Plutocratic Capitalism. The present form of Capitalism in the United States, sometimes called Free market capitalism or Laissez-faire capitalism is pure Plutocratic Capitalism.

Lastly, Advanced Technologies and Automation through machines and software that make life easier for humanity are here to stay, and their impact will be massive unemployment, much more severe than what we are seeing today. And this is great because such massive unemployment will free humanity to express its creativity instead of toiling for a living. Let's allow machines and software do the boring, mundane and dangerous jobs unfit for humans to handle. In short, any work that can be done efficiently by a machine or software should not be done by any human being.

You may thus be wondering how then the unemployed will survive or earn a salary to live. Well, we were not born to have jobs. Among all the animal species, we humans are the only ones that get jobs to earn a living in the form of money. Money should be a means to an end, not an end in itself. It was invented as a convenient tool for us to exchange our goods and services instead of trading by cumbersome barter.

We do not have to have jobs to earn a living. There is no natural law indicating so. This is where the wonder of the Revolutionary Democratic Capitalism comes in handy. We can eat our cake and have it back. We can get jobs if we choose to but if we don't, we can still earn significant incomes to make a difference in our lives and the lives of humanity as a whole.

More to come on this Revolutionary Democratic Capitalism in volumes II and III, but in the meantime, let's conclude this book by reiterating the most salient points in the Epilogue that follows.

EPILOGUE

We have now come to the end of the first Volume of this book, and I have given you the following factual information.

1. The Government is not the Nation.

2. The Nation's Budget is the combined Budgets of the Government, all Households and all Businesses within the Nation.

3. As such, the Nation's Budget Deficit is the combined Budget Deficits of the Government, all Households and all Businesses in the Nation.

4. Subsequently, the Government Budget Deficit is not the Nation's Budget Deficit

5. If the Government Budget Deficit is not the Nation's Budget Deficit, then the so-called Government Budget Deficit touted as the Nations' Budget Deficit is phony, a fraud.

6. Furthermore, the so-called Government Budget Deficit is not part of the Financial Statements and Double-Entry-Bookkeeping in Accounting. Rather, Government Revenues and Government Expenditures, from which the so-called Government Budget Deficit is derived are. They are simply part of the Credit and Debit of the Double-Entry Accounting System, applied to balance the core Accounting Equation, the Balance Sheet

Assets = Liabilities + Owner's Equity

7. As such, Revenues and Expenditures alone do not give the total picture of the financial health of a person, household, business or government. All four Financial Statements earlier in the book --- Balance sheet, Income Statement, Cash-flow Statement and

Shareholders' Equity Statement --- interacting and relating with one another, give the true economic health of an entity, especially a nation.

8. I also asserted and proved that,

Nation's Income = Nation's Expenditure

and this is the Formula that matters to all Nations and not the deadly Formula,

Government Income = Government Expenditure

These aside, I also asserted that

Real Nation's Deficit = Nation's Income – Nations Expenditure

where the Nation's Expenditure is greater than the Nation's Income and not,

Nation's Budget Deficit = Government Income – Government Expenditure

as in present conventional economics, where Government Expenditure is greater than Government Income.

9. Lastly, I briefly mentioned the most fundamental economics balancing equation or formula for all Nations,

Money in Circulation in the hands of Consumers = Real Wealth of goods and services

This Formula will be described in more detail in the upcoming Volume II of this book; and its relationship to the Formula,

Nation's Income = Nation's Expenditure

will be shown and proven.

Now, the Super-committee set up by the United States Congress to reduce the Government Budget Deficit (not the Nation's Real Deficit) chased a phantom for its duration. All their efforts came to naught because tit is extremely foolish to chase an illusion called Government Budget Deficit, touted as the Nation's Budget Deficit, if there is even anything like a Nation's Budget Deficit. Rather, there is a Real Nation's Deficit, which is the mismatch of the amount of money in circulation in the hands of Consumers compared to the goods and services already produced within the Nation. It is also the mismatch of the Nation's Income to the nation's Expenditure.

This Real Nation's Deficit will be explained more explicitly in Volume II of this book, and it is the solution to the present global recession, especially the one in the United States.

In the meantime, with this new knowledge you've acquired here, educate your families, friends, associates, congressmen, senators, the White House and any of the Budget Deficit Hawks, about the illusory and fraudulent Government Budget Deficit, to save the American economy and yourselves. Inform them that the so-called Government Budget Deficit is not just phony and a monumental fraud, but extremely dangerous, and presently destroying our total economy and our lives. In short,

There is nothing like Government Budget Deficit.

There is nothing like Nation's Budget Deficit

and hence,

There is nothing like Nation's Debt.

The only National Debt incurred by the United States is the cumulative Debt from our annual Trade Deficits with the rest of the world, especially China, and this has nothing to do with the so-called Government Budget Deficit or Nation's Budget Deficit. We are exporting less than we are importing and hence, the cumulative Trade Deficits we call our National or Nation's Debt.

Our Trade Deficits which are Trade Surpluses for foreign countries like China, help the Chinese purchase US Government Bond, and this brings up the economic or debtor/creditor relationship between the United States and China. How can a poor country like China with a 2011 GDP per Capita of $8,288.82, loan money to the United States with a 2011 GDP per Capita of $48,665.81?[1]

It simply does not add up and makes no sense. This scenario is occurring because of the same senseless, meaningless and useless Government Budget Deficit and National Debt reduction, or balancing the Government Budget and National Debt, in the name of fiscal prudence. A better nomenclature will be fiscal suicide.

Now, you know and if you do nothing, then you are also helping to destroy the American economy, yourselves and the future of generations of Americans.

Pass on this message. Educate your fellow Americans NOW, for your own good and for the good of every American including Americans unborn.

Finally, you can now ask the following questions posed at the beginning of this book, to the budget deficit hawks --- the economic gurus, the television pundits, your friends, your uncle, your neighbor, your legislators and all those who still believe in reducing the government budget deficit and national debt, with the ultimate intent of balancing the government budget and national debt.

1. Who invented the Government Budget Deficit and why?

2. How have you been hurt receiving money from the Government?

3. How have you been hurt by the Government reducing your taxes?

4. How have you been hurt by the Government spending money to repair our bridges, roads, and sewer systems, build new infrastructure, boost our education system and increase funding for research and development?

5. How have you or anyone you know been hurt by the Government Budget Deficit?

6. How is the Government Budget Deficit the most serious problem in the US today?

7. If the Government is not the Nation, why is the Government Budget Deficit the Nation's Budget Deficit?

8. Since the United States Congress sets the tax rates for all Americans and also decides how much money the Government can spend, why does the Congress not raise taxes high enough to match its expenditure? After all, Congress totally controls both component parameters of the Budget Deficit, Revenues and Expenditures.

9. Finally, what exactly is money and why do we make it scarce compared to our real wealth, being wasted in the form of foreclosed homes, unsold cars, empty offices, shuttered factories and unemployed professionals like engineers and lawyers? Why do we make money more important than life, when millions of Americans are homeless in the midst of hundreds of thousands or even a few million foreclosed and empty homes?

There will only be silence or nonsensical responses that have nothing to do with the so-called Government Budget Deficit or the real economy of production and services, to meet our human needs. For, there is nothing like Government Budget Deficit as an indicator of the economic health of any society. The Government Budget Deficit is a phantom, an outright fraud, and an extremely deadly one.

If the United States Congress wants to balance the phony Federal Budget Deficit or the so-called National Debt, all it needs to do is print enough money to match its annual Budget and the amount of the useless National Debt. Very simple and straight forward. As long as the amount of printed money in circulation in the hands of Real Consumers match the Real Wealth of goods and services on our shelves, the much feared inflation will not rear its head. The phony Government Budget Deficit and phantom National Debt are mere shenanigans and irrelevant to the overall United States Economy.

What matters most is for the Government of the United States to focus on the Real National Deficit, the shortfall of money in the hands of Real Consumers to buy up the Real Wealth on our shelves. This is the only way to end this Great Recession and start an Economic Recovery. In short, the White House, US Congress and the Fed must match the amount of Money in Circulation in the hands of Real Consumers with the goods and services we have already produced, or

Money in Circulation in   =   Real Wealth of goods
the hands of Consumers   and services

That's all.

More factually fascinating and exhilarating information coming in Volumes II and III, each Volume a continuation of the previous. In other words, Volume III starts where Volume II ends and Volume

II starts where this Volume I ended. Stay tuned for more excitement and scintillation as we usher ourselves into the 21st Century Knowledge Economy in concert with the Revolutionary Democratic Capitalism, where having a job to earn an income is no longer the norm. In fact, unemployment becomes a non-issue

ABOUT THE AUTHOR

Bright Harry is presently writing four books at the same time and on accelerated schedule. You have the first one in your hands right at this moment, entitled "America, Wake Up! We are Destroying the American Economy and Ourselves. The urgency of the present Global economic mess, especially in the United States, prompted him to push forward the completion schedule. The other three books are "The Deadliest Formula in the World", "The Government is not the Nation", and "Revolutionary Democratic Capitalism (Economic System of the 21st Century and Beyond). The essence of all four books is to solve once and for all, the present Global Economic meltdown and calamitous wealth discrimination that are destroying billions of lives, creating massively unbelievable poverty, and causing and exacerbating terrorism all around the world.

He is a Mechanical Engineer by profession with a minor in business and economics. As previous founder and CEO of several High Technology Companies in Silicon Valley, he has a pulse of the business world and now putting his pragmatic ideas in writing to make the world much better, while helping humanity as a whole. His focus and writings are usually on technology, business strategies and modern economics.

His present and immediate goal is to prevent the US Congress and the White House from turning the Great Recession of 2007 into the Great Depression of the 21st Century through ignorance, as was the case between 1929 and 1932.

His ultimate goal is the replacement of the presently flawed Feudalistic and Plutocratic Capitalism of the United States with the transformative Democratic Capitalism ensconced in an Economic Democracy that is always intertwined with its twin

Political Democracy, for us to continue being the beacon of light and visionary Nation to the rest of the world.

You can get the latest information on this book, "America, Wake Up! We are Destroying the American Economy and Ourselves", at his Website, AmericaWakeUpSite.com.

MY GLOBAL CHALLENGE

If any human being on this earth can disprove the following assertions or postulations I have propounded in this Volume I of this book, I will pay the first person who does it, my first $25,000 profit from the sale of this book. Here are the postulations.

The Government is not the Nation,

Hence,

Government Budget is not the Nation's Budget

Government Budget Deficit is not the Nation's Budget Deficit

Government Debt is not the Nation's Debt

Furthermore,

Government Income is not the National Income

Government Expenditure is also not the National Expenditure

As such,

there is no National Budget Deficit

and

there is no National Debt

Yes! the first person who disproves the above postulations will be given the first $25,000 from the profits I make from this book of mine.

I have already proven in this first Volume that there is nothing like Government Budget Deficit since the Government can always print enough money to match its expenditure, instead of imposing unnecessary taxes for such a purpose. Taxes are a necessary evil

We are Destroying the American Economy and Ourselves

for redistribution of income and wealth, to prevent disruptive Income and Wealth discrimination, but not to reduce a phony Federal Budget Deficit or to balance a fraudulent Government Debt touted as National Debt.

You can send your information debunking my above postulations through my Website,

http://www.americawakeupsite.com/html/challenge.html

Once at the Site, complete the form but ensure that you have thoroughly read and understood the whole book and the contents on the Website before responding. In this way, we do not waste each other's time and energy.

NOTES

The following Notes show the sources of information, the superscript numbers and corresponding pages showing where they can be found in the book.

No.   Page

Chapter 1

1   Gramm-Rudman-Hollings Balanced Budget Act.   17
http://en.wikipedia.org/wiki/Gramm%E2%80%93Rudman
%E2%80%93Hollings_Balanced_Budget_Act

2   Summary of the Revised Budget Control Act of 2011.   21
http://www.speaker.gov/News/DocumentSingle.aspx?
DocumentID=254628

Chapter 2

1   Franklin D. Roosevelt, Nomination Address at the   25
Democratic National Convention of 1932 (July 2, 1932)

2   President Obama defending his 2012 budget proposal   26
amid criticism from Republicans on February 15, 2011
http://abcnews.go.com/Politics/obama-defends-2012-
budget-addresses-deficit-tax-overhaul/story?id=12921014

3   President Obama during his weekly on July 23, 2011,   26
ahead of an emergency meeting at the White House.
http://www.msnbc.msn.com/id/43864749/ns/politics-
capitol_hill/

4   President Barack Obama's Monday evening, July 25,   27
2011, address on the debt ceiling impasse in
Washington DC
http://www.msnbc.msn.com/id/43888713/ns/politics-
capitol_hill/t/obamas-full-address-debt-ceiling-
impasse/#.TptX3nKxztQ

America, Wake Up!

We are Destroying the American Economy and Ourselves

Chapter 8

Epilogue